Contemporary Political Movements and the Thought of Jacques Rancière

Equality in Action

Todd May

EDINBURGH UNIVERSITY PRESS

© Todd May, 2010

Edinburgh University Press Ltd
22 George Square, Edinburgh

www.euppublishing.com

Typeset in 11/13pt Adobe Sabon
by Servis Filmsetting Ltd, Stockport, Cheshire, and
printed and bound in Great Britain by
CPI Antony Rowe, Chippenham and Eastbourne

A CIP record for this book is available from the British Library

ISBN 978 0 7486 3982 3 (hardback)
ISBN 978 0 7486 3983 0 (paperback)

Contents

Preface

This book is the product of a particular kind of hope. The left as an organized force in the United States and to a lesser extent Europe is in disarray. Throughout the eight years of outrages perpetrated by the Bush administration, there was surprisingly little organized struggle by people of a progressive bent. The prospects for the near future are hardly brighter, even if the immediate electoral situation in the US has improved somewhat. (It is difficult to imagine how it could have gotten worse.)

And yet, our world seems never without movements that struggle for and through real democracy. They enact in their deeds a world that many of us can only give shape to with our words. It is from these movements, and often from the courage and integrity of the people participating in them, that I draw that particular kind of hope.

My previous book on Jacques Rancière's political thought sought to articulate a framework from within which we could conceive democratic political movements. It was largely theoretical in character. Here I turn my attention to several specific movements that have arisen over the past couple of decades, seeking to show how many of the insights he has offered help us understand their dynamics and point a way toward conceiving progressive political action. Understanding, of course, is not a substitute for action. But it may serve as a way of reflecting on that action, and of giving form to our vision of the future.

There are many people to thank for their assistance in this project, starting with M. Rancière himself, who encouraged me to pursue it when I presented it to him as a possible avenue for developing his ideas. A number of others have helped me realize it, and for that, I am grateful. Without their generosity, this book, flawed as it is, could not have been written. In addition, without the assistance of Carol Macdonald and Máiréad McElligott and two anonymous readers at Edinburgh University press, this book would not have been available for reading; and without the copy-editing of Anna Oxbury would not have been readable.

I would also like to thank the editors at the Canadian philosophical journal *Symposium* and at *Anarchist Studies*. The first and second chapters respectively are developments of articles that previously appeared in those journals.

Finally, I would like to dedicate this book to my family: Kathleen, David, Rachel, and Joel. They sustain me.

Thinking Politics with Jacques Rancière

It is the task of the left to think and act upon democracy. In many ways, it has always been the task of the left to do so, even though we have often failed at that task. Conservatism by its nature seeks to resist change, or at best to allow change to happen slowly. Change, for conservatives, must always happen within the parameters of tradition. But democracy has never been on the side of tradition. Tradition favors those in power. Democracy is about everyone, not simply those in power. Democracy almost always is a challenge to tradition. That is why its creation is a task belonging to the left.

This does not mean that the right does not refer to democracy. In fact, there is a lot of talk about democracy these days coming from many quarters. Much of this talk is, unsurprisingly, pretty elitist. The most obvious example of this elitism is in the discourse of the recent Bush administration in the United States. We in the US were told that our God-given mission was to bring democracy to places that lack it. This was especially true of those places that have a lot of oil. For some reason, oil seems to require more democracy than other natural resources. The character of this oil-driven democracy, obvious and banal as it is, should not escape our notice. Democracy is a system of elections and capitalist economics that revolves around ceding political and economic power to those who know best how to utilize that power. Democracy, in this view, is an agreement between those who are governed and who work on the one hand, and those who govern them and who control their workplaces on the other. It is an agreement that all of this is a very good arrangement.

It is perhaps no surprise that many places in the world that have been subject to that arrangement, perhaps most especially in the Middle East and in Central and South America, have periodically wondered about it, and are wondering about it once again. Of course, they have good historical reason to wonder. The Bush administration was not the first US administration to intervene into the affairs of others in the name of democracy. The US has a venerable history of "democratic" intervention, one that stands alongside, even if it does not rival, that of Europe.

This book is about democracy, but not about the democracy envisioned by the elites. It is about democracy as a challenge to the way we are often told democracy works. It is about democracy as it concerns people who are not in power, rather than as a buttress for people who are. Therefore, we will not speak of elections here, nor of the virtues of the free market. We will, instead, study movements that seek to create democracy from the ground up, movements of what was once called – and will perhaps again be called – the people.

There are two reasons to study such movements, particularly among those who seek democracy and democratic change. The first is to understand how they work. What is it that democratic movements do? Wherein does their democratic character lie? How does resistance to those movements operate, and how have those movements responded? By studying current or recent movements that merit the label *democratic*, we can learn about what can and cannot be done in our world by those who are not favored by the power-holders.

The second reason to study such movements is less analytic. It concerns hope.

We on the left, particularly in the US and Europe, have political hope in short supply these days. A cynic might say that people in the first world can afford to limit the supply of hope, because we have supplies of so much else. I reject this view. I believe it gets things backwards. True, there is an apathy that seems to affect us and keep us from political action. And it may seem as though that apathy has diminished the hope necessary for political resistance. However, our hopelessness is not based on apathy. It is the other way around. It is because people don't know how to intervene, what to do, that they begin to appear not to care. Apathy is the symptom. It is hopelessness that is the cause.

People who seek to create democracy today are in a much more difficult situation than people were a generation ago. When I was growing up during the 1960s, the issues were clear. In the US, civil rights and the Vietnam War topped the agenda. What could be clearer than the equality of African Americans and the need to stop sending Americans to Vietnam to attack its people? (One might say that Iraq is like Vietnam, and it may become so. But the absence of a draft and the unwillingness of the media to report the horrors we have created there make it less visible to many of us.) Today, globalization and the domination of the media have made intervention more difficult even while it has become more urgent. We cast about for models or examples of resistance, and we find ourselves bereft. We are called, and we often call ourselves, apathetic. But this is only because we don't know where and how to look, where and how to go about creating democracy.

By writing primarily about democratic political movements, I try to address here both the question of how to think about democracy and the obstacles to hope. Regarding the first, my own hope is to offer some examples of how democratic movements can work, examples that may have relevance or resonance for those today who want to create a politics of the left. Regarding the second, it follows from the first. By appealing to examples, I want to show that democracy is still an option in our world. There are those who, in various ways and in various places, seek to create democracy. They seek to create it not by toppling governments and installing capitalism, but by acting in their own names and in the names of those they care about. If this book succeeds, it is because it at once offers a framework for thinking about current democratic movements and the hope that they are still possible.

If one is seeking examples of democratic movements, however, one must first ask what one is looking for. The philosopher Socrates knew this dilemma. How, he asked, will we know we have found what we're looking for if we don't know what it is in the first place? This chapter offers a view of what it is in the first place. It seeks to answer the question of how to think about democracy, utilizing the work of the contemporary French theorist and historian Jacques Rancière. I have recently written a more theoretically oriented book engaging with his conception of democracy.[1] Here, however, I want only to offer a general framework, one that will answer Socrates' question. My interest here is in giving a picture of the democracy we're looking for, so that when we run across it in the chapters that follow, we can recognize what we're seeing. In those chapters, I will try to draw out various implications of what is said here, with reference to their appearance in specific political movements.

If we turn our attention from public policy to the academy, we find that there is elitism not only in our leaders but in theories. There is an elitism at the heart of philosophical reflection on democracy, an elitism I would like to take a moment to expose before turning toward a view of democracy that turns against it. This elitism lies, ironically, in the use to which the concept of equality is put. The theorist Amartya Sen remarks, rightly in my view, that "a common characteristic of virtually all the approaches to the ethics of social arrangements that have stood the test of time is to want the equality of *something* – something that has an important place in the particular theory."[2] We can locate this idea not only in his views, but in those of all the major traditional liberal democratic theorists. It is the central project of recent liberal theories of justice to answer the question of what kind of equality is to be distributed, and how. Thus, there is at the heart of the liberal project a democratic equality.

And yet, at the heart of this democratic equality, there lies an elitism. What those in this tradition do not question in their disagreements about what type of equality people deserve is a presupposition informing the question they seek to answer. There is general agreement that equality is, first and foremost, a matter of what people deserve. Otherwise put, it is a matter of what they should receive. This is why these theories are often called *distributive* theories. Distributive theories address what kinds of distributions ought to be made of the social goods. To think about equality, as these theories do, in terms of distribution has at least two implications we should reject.

First, distribution implies a distributor. Once the type of equality to be distributed is decided upon, the distributor is responsible for ensuring both the distribution and the maintenance of the proper distribution. Most often, this distributor is the state, although it need not be.

Second, following from this, distribution implies a passivity on the part of those who receive the distribution. The people living in a particular society do not, unless they form part of the distributing class, have anything to do with equality other than to be the object of it.

We can readily see the politics of traditional liberalism at work in these implications. Taken together, they help sustain a hierarchical view of society in which the members of that society are conceived as individuals pursuing disparate and unrelated ends that the state helps them more or less to achieve.

There is, then, a thread that connects the elitism of traditional liberal theory with the more cynical uses to which it is put by various administrations in the US and Europe particularly. The game is given away at the outset. Once you posit the idea that equality is to be distributed, then the only questions left are those of which equality and how most efficiently to get it to people. There is a hierarchical order in which those who are the object of equality are not its subject. And, of course, if there is such a hierarchical order then there isn't really equality.

Some who read this will want to point out that the inequality at issue here, at least in liberal theory, is only administrative. While it might be true that real politics involves hierarchies of power, liberal theory delegates only the power to administrate distributive equality to those in political office. It is the job of political institutions to ensure that whatever equality is decided upon is actually distributed to people. And while it may be the case that those who act in the name of liberal theory are not limited to administrative roles – they seek, and often obtain, real power – this is not the fault of the theories. Liberal theories, it will be said, provide an adequate framework for thinking about equality, even if its practitioners fall short.

Unfortunately, this will not work. One response to this defense of liberal theories would be to point out that a type of theory that is regularly violated in its own name is probably not a very good basis for thinking about political arrangements. That seems to me to be a good response. But the problem lies deeper. It is not only a matter of the relationship between liberal theory and political practice. There is a problem in the theory itself. Once people are thought to be objects of distribution rather than subjects of creation, then hierarchy is inevitable. The idea that those who distribute equality are simply performing an administrative task hides a deeper problem. It divides people into those who are politically active and those who are politically passive. And to be politically passive is not to be equal, in the creation of one's own life, to those who are active.

How might we think about equality in a non-hierarchical fashion? How might equality be conceived with some degree of, well, equality? The problem with the two presuppositions of liberalism is that, by distributing equality, they place most people at the receiving end of the political operation. There are those who distribute equality, and those who receive it. Once you start with that assumption, the hierarchy is already in place. It's too late to return to equality. Equality, instead of being the result of a political process, must be conceived as the *presupposition* of those who act. It must be the expression of political actors rather than the possession of a political hierarchy. In the formulation of Jacques Rancière, whose ideas form the framework of my thinking in this book, "Politics only happens when these mechanisms [to be described below] are stopped in their tracks by the effect of a presupposition that is totally foreign to them yet without which none of them could ultimately function: the presupposition of the equality of anyone and everyone."[3]

Rancière's political and aesthetic views are beginning to take hold in political thought in the English-speaking world, especially in the wake of the spate of recent translations of his work. However, they are still unfamiliar to many people. Before turning to the use I would like to make of them, it would perhaps be best to offer a quick, if a bit sketchy, overview of his political thought. And to start, it is perhaps worth noting that Rancière had been a student of Marxist theorist Louis Althusser's, but then repudiated his teacher in the wake of the events of May '68.[4] Althusser was a structuralist Marxist. In his earlier writings, he emphasizes Marxism as a science, one that requires an avant-garde party that understands the workings of capitalism, as well as its structural weak points that allow for intervention. Although he later softens this position, seeing philosophy not so much as a science but as a theoretical element of class struggle, in Rancière's eyes Althusser never repudiates the distinction, based on division of labor, between intellectuals and workers.

The events of May 1968, which helped form the intellectual orientation of many recent French thinkers, such as Michel Foucault, Gilles Deleuze, and Jean-François Lyotard, also had its effect on Rancière. Although we cannot recount those events here, the key element for Rancière and many others was the way in which those events unfolded from below, led by students and workers rather than by those chosen (or self-chosen) to lead them.[5] When the French Communist Party repudiated the uprising, Rancière came face to face with its hierarchical character, and especially the division of labor it posited between those, like Althusser, whose job is to think and to formulate theory and projects, and those others – the workers – whose job is merely to carry out the projects of the thinkers. Rancière then broke with Althusser, immersed himself in archives of nineteenth-century worker writings,[6] and eventually formulated a view of political action that focuses on the presupposition of equality.

How might we conceive this equality out of which people act? Is there some sort of content to the presupposition of equality, or is the term *equality* merely a rhetorical device to motivate political action? In Rancière's thought, the idea of equality can be an elusive one. This is because, on the one hand, he wants to resist assimilating it to any form of identity politics. (Identity politics, which locates struggles along various registers of identity, ex. blackness, women, queerness, will be discussed in more detail in Chapter 4.) On the other hand, however, he does give it some content. In his major theoretical text *Disagreement* he often refers to equality in terms of an "empty freedom" that everyone possesses.[7] That might lead one to believe that there is nothing to the concept of equality. There is a way in which this is right. There is nothing to the concept of equality that would distinguish any particular group of people from any other group. There are no particular qualities one possesses that make one equal to others. In other words, politics cannot rely on an essence, whether it be blackness, the feminine, an indigenous character, etc., out of which it emerges. Politics is not the protection of particular qualities or the expression of particular essences. Equality, as Rancière says, is an equality of anyone and everyone.

This does not mean that the empty freedom of which he speaks is entirely without content. The equality that is presupposed in political action is a certain equality of intelligence. In an earlier text, *The Ignorant Schoolmaster*, Rancière tells the story of Joseph Jacotot, a refugee from post-Revolutionary France, who found himself in Flanders trying to teach a group of students who only knew Flemish, while he could only speak French. Working with a dual-language copy of a single text, he assigned his students to write a paper on the text in French. When they turned in their assignments, it emerged that their papers were of excellent quality. Jacotot decided that all people were of equal intelligence; differences in performance stemmed from inability to attend rather than from innate intellectual differences. And, furthermore, these latter stemmed in turn from the presupposition inculcated in many students that they were of lesser intelligence.

The assumption that people are of equal intelligence does not need to be a fine-grained one. In other words, it does not require that we hold people to be equally capable of doing high-level theoretical physics or solving difficult mathematical problems. What Jacotot – or at least Rancière's Jacotot – is after is more concrete, especially with regard to politics. We are, unless we are deeply damaged in some way, capable of creating meaningful lives with one another, talking with one another, understanding one another, and reasoning about ourselves and our situations. Our social and political contexts, while sometimes difficult and complex, do not involve essential mysteries that we are in principle incapable of comprehending without the assistance of a savant of some sort. They may be difficult to understand, and require reflection and study. One cannot assume one understands, for instance, the workings of globalization without reading and thinking about it. But, and this is the key point, there is nothing *essentially* hidden that cannot be understood by almost all of us. There is no psychoanalytic unconscious or self-masking structural element or concealing of Being that makes it impossible for one to grasp (at least more or less) one's self and one's situation and that therefore requires an expert or an intellectual to decode.

In short, we are capable of formulating and carrying out our lives with one another. This, in Rancière's view, is the assumption – the presupposition of equality – with which politics begins. "[O]ur problem isn't proving that all intelligence is equal. It's seeing what can be done under that presupposition. And for this, it's enough for us that the opinion be possible – that is, that no opposing truth be proved."[8]

For some, even this much might seem overly optimistic. After all, given the wide range of intellectual capacities that seem to be on display, isn't it a stretch to think of people as equally intelligent? Furthermore, from a leftist perspective, how is one to explain the prevalence of people who seem to embrace policies and leaders who work consistently against their interest? Aren't people fairly easily duped? And if so, isn't the assumption of equal intelligence a thin reed upon which to rest a democratic politics?

We must understand what the equality of intelligence implies. It does not mean that people cannot be misled, or that people's intellectual capacities are entirely overlapping. It means something simpler: that people can understand themselves and their world enough to create meaningful lives together. I would argue that this assumption is not only possible, but that it is *necessary* for any progressive politics. To see why, imagine that one were to operate a politics on the assumption that people were *not* equally intelligent in this minimal sense. What would be the point of liberation then? It would make no sense to liberate people from social hierarchies if they were incapable of conducting their own lives with one another. The best one could hope for would be a less egregious hierarchy, a sort of paternalist government that would take care of people who, in the end, were incapable of taking care of themselves. It seems, then, that what Rancière has embraced as the content of the presupposition of equality is not a controversial notion of equal intelligence but the very assumption animating all progressive politics. He has merely brought it out into the open and made it the founding presupposition of his political thought.

The difficulty faced by those who embrace the presupposition of equality is precisely that societies, instead of being arranged on the basis of that presupposition, are instead arranged on the opposite one. Societies are hierarchically ordered. Roles are distributed on the presupposition that certain people are just not as intelligent as others. Think, for instance, of the history of gender or racial relations. Think of the assumptions made by managers about the inherent limits of worker ability. The divisions between intellectual and manual labor, between the private and the public sphere, between the government and the governed, are guided by a hierarchy founded in the presupposition of inequality. One of the reasons we find it so difficult to imagine another social order is that these hierarchies present themselves as natural or inescapable, because the presupposition of *in*equality has become ingrained in us.

These hierarchical orderings, and the principles that guide and justify them, are often called politics. Rancière proposes instead to call them the police. "Politics is generally seen as the set of procedures whereby the aggregation and consent of collectivities is achieved, the organization of powers, the distribution of places and roles, and the systems for legitimizing this distribution. I propose to give this system of distribution another name. I propose to call it *the police*."[9] In utilizing the term police, Rancière makes it clear that he is not simply thinking of folks in uniform with truncheons and guns. "Michel Foucault has shown that, as a mode of government, the police described by writers of the seventeenth and eighteenth centuries covered everything relating to 'man' and his 'happiness.'"[10] Rancière is referring here to a series of lectures given by Foucault in 1978 entitled *Security, Territory, Population*.[11] In those lectures, Foucault traces the rise of the science of police, particularly in Germany, in the seventeenth century. The science of police concerns the government's oversight of the various aspects of a population: health, welfare, birth rates, etc. The idea is that with the rise of national states and national economic requirements, governments had to take account of and intervene upon the character of a nation's society.

The police, then, refers broadly to the structure and justification of a social hierarchy. Furthermore, a point that will be central to Rancière's later works on aesthetics, the police order is also a matter of how we perceive ourselves, one another, and our world. It consists in a partition or division of the sensible, a *partage du sensible*. (We will return to this phrase below.) There is a partitioning not solely of social space but also of our perception of things that reinforces social hierarchies.

On this view much of what passes for politics, much of what we think of as politics, is simply policing. This does not mean that all policing is equally bad. A police order that refuses to educate people of a certain race or ethnicity or one that denies support to poor people is worse than a police order that functions otherwise. The distinction Rancière draws between the police and politics is not drawn simply along the normatively bad–normatively good axis. While politics is better than policing, there are normative degrees within police orders themselves.

There is a problem, however, with confusing politics, or what we will come to call for the sake of clarity *democratic politics*, with policing. If we think that politics ends with the proper orientation of police functions, with what traditional theorists call distributive justice, then we have stifled our political possibilities. We have limited political involvement to elections, lobbying, and otherwise obeying. We are encouraged to think of politics this way. We are told that it is our duty to vote, and that it is our duty to respect the outcome of elections and obey those in power. We are told that the alpha and omega of politics is what Rancière calls policing.

But what might politics be if it is an activity beyond policing?

> I . . . propose to reserve the term *politics* for an extremely determined activity antagonistic to policing: whatever breaks with the tangible configuration whereby parties and parts or lack of them are defined by a presupposition that, by definition, has no place in that configuration – that of the part that has no part . . . political activity is always a mode of expression that undoes the perceptible divisions of the police order by implementing a basically heterogeneous assumption, that of the part who have no part, an assumption that, at the end of the day, itself demonstrates the contingency of the order, the equality of any speaking being with any other speaking being.[12]

Politics concerns what Rancière calls *the part who have no part*, or, as he sometimes puts it, *the count of the uncounted*. Who are those who have no part or are uncounted? They are those who, in a particular social arrangement (or in one aspect of it), are thought less than equal to others. They are the blacks, women, the indigenous, workers, those who have no part to play in deciding the shape of the police order, because they are inferior. And politics consists in disrupting the police order that excludes or marginalizes them through the assertion, often both in word and in deed, of their equality in that police order. That assertion, that *heterogeneous assumption*, disrupts the police order by showing its contingency. There is no reason why those on top are over here and those on the bottom or outside are over there. That arrangement is due to the contingencies of history rather than the necessities of nature. Politics is the assertion of equality among those who presuppose it among themselves.

If we presuppose the equal intelligence of everyone, then it must be a matter of contingency if one person or group winds up higher in a hierarchy than another. The presupposition is precisely that everyone can conduct a meaningful life alongside others. Therefore, the ability of some to police the lives of others cannot be a matter of superior intelligence. There is no necessity to their being where they are. Those who have a part, who count, do not deserve their part in contrast to those who don't. This is an idea that is difficult to get comfortable with, since so much of what we are taught reinforces the idea that those in power (whether economic, political, domestic, or otherwise) deserve to be there, and the rest of us do not. As Rancière tells us, "From Athens in the fifth century BC up until our own governments, the party of the rich has only ever said one thing, which is most precisely the negation of politics: there is no part of those who have no part."[13]

But if we assume "the equality of any speaking being with any other speaking being," then we must recognize at once the contingency of any police order, any order that justifies a hierarchy and that allows some to think that their unequal status relative to others is justified. It would seem that this is the only way for equality to work if it is to be a presupposition rather than a distribution.

If equality were to offer another, better set of roles for people to play, it would merely be a matter of social distribution, akin to what liberal theorists have offered. But that is not, in Rancière's view, how equality should work. By presupposing equality in the face of a police order, roles are subverted, not just rearranged. "The essence of equality is in fact not so much to unify as to declassify, to undo the supposed naturalness of orders and replace it with the controversial figures of division."[14] There are, for instance, no blacks, neither in the sense that racists would have it of an inferior people nor in the sense of identity politics that there is a blackness that must be respected and expressed. There may be people with darker or lighter skin tones than others, but for the purpose of politics this is entirely irrelevant. It matters only that they are equal.

This is not to say that a group cannot pull itself together under a certain name to assert its equality. There can be, in some sense, a black movement, or what South African leader Steven Biko called a Black Consciousness Movement. But in such movements, one must be careful. A black movement is not a movement that has deep roots in blackness. It may have deep roots in how those with darker skin have been treated, or in the practices that they have developed historically under the yoke of that treatment. But this is a double-edged sword, one that probably cuts the wrong way more sharply than one would like. To take on the categories of blackness – like queerness, and other-*nesses* – is to ratify a part of the history of one's own oppression. Many people have argued that if one takes on that history defiantly rather than meekly, one turns the oppression on its head. "Yes, I am black." "Yes, I am queer," one announces without apology. That, of course, is the road of identity politics. Its history has, more often than not, failed to be an inspiring one. Better, Rancière argues, to abandon the labels rather than seek to turn them to one's own use. The project of a democratic politics is not the unification of a group of people under a particular label, but their declassification from the identities of the police order.

This is not to say that a democratic politics is not in any way unifying. It must unify, since it involves collective action. The form of unification it involves is that a collective subject is formed through collective action. He calls this formation of a collective subject *subjectification*. "By subjectification I mean the production through a series of actions of a body and a capacity for enunciation not previously identifiable within a given field of experience, whose identification is thus part of the reconfiguration of the field of experience."[15] What exactly does this mean? That through democratic political action a collective subject arises. This collective subject speaks in the name (or at least from the presupposition of) its equality and in so speaking becomes recognized as a particular collective subject.

For example, recently in the United States immigrants, both legal and illegal, are coming together and speaking against the discrimination and bigotry they often face. Their doing so has several consequences. First, they become a collective subject. Second, through their collective speech, they become recognized as a collective subject. Before recent immigrant action, in the minds of many Americans there were only individuals, and not even those. These individuals were not so much people as dark forces that sought to undermine the US economy and its security. As people, they were largely invisible. However, recent demonstrations have made them visible as people and as a collective subject. This has had the further effect of changing the experience many non-immigrants have of them. In Rancière's terms, it has reconfigured the field of experience for many Americans. We will see in the next chapter an immigrant movement in Montréal that has had much the same effect, and in addition has had important political success. And we will investigate in greater depth the dynamic of subjectification in the third chapter, where we discuss the first Palestinian intifada.

For the moment, however, it is important to distinguish subjectification from identity politics. It is not that subjectification does not involve a name or some sort of self-identification. What is important is the particular inflection this name or this self-identification takes. Rancière draws the distinction between subjectification and the kind of identity he seeks to avoid this way. "The difference that political disorder inscribes in the police order can thus, at first glance, be expressed as the difference between subjectification and identification. It inscribes a subject name as being different from any identified part of the community."[16] Subjectification refuses to take up the identifications that are on the menu of the current police order. In essence, then, subjectification does not repeat the names of a police order; it creates its own name.

But in creating its own name, it divorces itself from any of the characteristics associated with it by the police order. To return to the example of a moment ago, the collective subject formed by immigrant demonstrations and declarations refuses to endorse any of the characteristics associated with "illegal immigrants" by much of the US population. In the name of what does this refusal take place? Not in the name of a particular identity or essence, but instead in the name of equality. And here is where the difference in inflection between Rancière's politics and a politics of identity lies. In the latter case, it is the substitution of one identity for another that forms the basis of the collective subject. In subjectification as Rancière describes it, it is instead equality that forms that basis. Rancière offers his own examples: "when the demonstrators in the Paris of 1968 declared, against all police evidence, 'We are all German Jews', they exposed for all to see the gap between political subjectification . . . and any kind of identification."[17]

On the surface, Rancière's perspective may sound like a variation, if perhaps with a more socialist bent, on liberalism. After all, doesn't he start from the presupposition of the equality of intelligence and then argue that people should all be treated the same way? And isn't this a form of liberalism? Doesn't liberalism want to abstract us from any particular qualities, see each of us as individuals, and then design a state or set of institutions that ensures that we are equally treated as such? This, however, is not what Rancière does. The addressee of his discourse is not the state or its institutions; it is the people, what he sometimes calls the *demos*, the part that has no part, or the uncounted. His proposal does not answer the question of how people ought to be treated by the state; it is not a distributive theory of justice. Rather, it concerns how people ought to act if they are to act democratically. In that sense, the entire structure of his discourse diverges from liberal theory.

Liberal theory, we might say, is top-down. It starts from the state, and asks how people should be treated by it. Rancière's approach to democratic politics is bottom-up. It starts from the people who engage in political action, and sees changes in the state (or the economy, or the family, etc.) as resulting from that.

By shifting his attention from the state to the people or the demos, some might see the hand of the German theorist Jürgen Habermas at work. The Habermasian picture is something like this. We are to regard everyone as equally intelligent. Thus, everyone should have an equal say in dictating the norms of the polity. This equal say, of course, is not a matter of one person, one vote. Rather, it is a matter of allowing the best reasons to emerge for the policy norms that are proposed. Is that not what it means to treat people as equally intelligent – not to take them at their word but to consider them as interlocutors in a search for reasonable norms? Isn't that how we should read Rancière when he writes that, "Reason begins when discourses organized with the goal of being right cease, begins where equality is recognized: not an equality decreed by law or force, not a passively received equality, but an equality in act, verified, at each step by those marchers who, in their constant attention to themselves and in their endless revolving around the truth, find the right sentences to make themselves understood by others"?[18]

There is something appealing in Habermas' work that distinguishes it from much work in the liberal tradition. This should not be entirely surprising, since Habermas comes from the Frankfurt School, a group of critical theorists including Theodor Adorno and Max Horkheimer who worked within a broadly Marxist tradition. In contrast to liberal thinkers, for whom the social contract is a theoretical entity, Habermas envisions a social contract actually being constructed by those involved in the polity. What Habermas seeks to do is to ask how to construct, not specific policies, but the norms by which specific policies should be made. It's not that everyone gets to decide on every issue that faces the social group. Rather, everyone gets to decide, through a reasonable exchange of views, the norms by which those decisions should be made. Those norms may, in keeping with liberal theory, be distributive ones. But they need not be.

Can we read this kind of bottom-up approach in Rancière's work?

What this reading of Rancière's work misses, however, is that the purpose of politics is not, as Habermas would have it, consensus. It is what Rancière calls *dissensus*, that is, a dissent from a given police order. "The essence of politics is the manifestation of dissensus, as the presence of two worlds in one."[19] Habermas, writing in the contractarian tradition, sees people in a situation abstracted from their real conditions. In fact, he would like to bring these people together, outside those conditions, in order to have them discuss the norms that would govern the conditions into which they would be placed. Thus, consensus would precede the concrete society in which one is to live, since it must be on the basis of such a consensus that a society is to be constructed.

Rancière's project is wholly different. His thought does not take place in a context outside of or abstracted from social conditions. Even when, as in *Disagreement*, he refers less often to *particular* social conditions, the starting point for his reflections is always the fact that politics must take place from within those conditions. There is always a situation, always a police, always a particular *partage du sensible*, a partition of the sensible. Politics is not a consensus about a particular partition of the sensible; it is a dissensus from it.

Here we begin to glimpse a relation that can be drawn between Rancière's conception of equality and the embrace of difference common to much recent French philosophy. In contrast to liberal theory, equality is not a matter of distributing the same. In contrast to Habermas, it is not a matter of coming to consensus. If people are equally intelligent and are to act out of the presupposition of that equal intelligence, it is neither to confirm any particular identity nor to propose one. It is instead to refuse the identities that are on offer, the roles that have been proffered by the current police arrangement. To put the point another way, it is not in the name of an identity or of a sameness that equality is acted out; it is in the name of difference. Equality, as Rancière tells us, does not unify; it declassifies. The "heterogeneous assumption" that politics offers is not simply a matter of an assumption with a different conceptual content – that of the equality of intelligence – but, following from that, a heterogeneity to the established police order that is not recuperable in the form of a different police order.

There is a particular affinity of such thought with that of, say, Jacques Derrida's reflections on democracy. Like Derrida, Rancière keeps democracy under the banner of a declassification rather than an identity. And like Derrida, the banner of declassification serves to preserve an equality that goes missing in traditional liberal theory. However, Rancière's approach to this declassification reveals an elitism in Derrida's thought as well. It is different kind of elitism from that of traditional liberal theory. Rather than an elitism of hierarchical structure it is what might be called an elitism of theoretical comfort. Since it would take us too far afield to develop this idea, I can only gesture at it here.

For Derrida, democracy can never coincide with itself. It is always to come, never here. In that sense, Derrida's democracy is anti-utopian. It doesn't envision an end to struggle, a point at which democracy is ever achieved. But this is not simply because it is an ideal that cannot be reached. This to-come is not simply a deferral into the future. It is a deferral *from itself* at every moment. As Derrida puts the point in his extended reflection on democracy, *Rogues*, "The 'to-come' not only points to the promise but suggests that a democracy will never exist, in the sense of a present existence: not because it will be deferred but because it will always remain aporetic in its structure."[20] He emphasizes that this aporia, this gap from itself, does not imply any sort of passivity. Rather, it implies both an acting toward and a self-critical stance. Democracy becomes that which guides our action but which must remain open as a guiding concept, lest we fall into the trap of deciding what it is and how it is to be imposed.

The animating thought here is that if we seek to bring the very concept of democracy into our conceptual grasp – that is, if we eliminate the aporia – we run the risk of a certain kind of totalitarianism. What kind of totalitarianism is this? In order to understand that, we must bear in mind that Derrida, as a writer in Europe, is intimately familiar with not only the legacy of fascism but also that of Stalinist communism. His works reflect the worry that at some point another revolution will come along and proclaim that it has achieved democracy. And what happens to those who do not fit the mold of democratic man or woman that is supposed to inhabit this achieved society? In the former Soviet Union, the gulags provided the answer.

Democracy that is claimed to be achieved is, for Derrida, a recipe for exclusion. It fails to recognize those who do not fit its mold. Therefore, the solution is to keep the very concept of democracy open, to keep it aporetic. This way, if we can put it like this, by not closing itself off nobody is left outside.

Derrida's approach avoids the problem of hierarchy inherent in traditional liberal theory. But it does so at the cost of being pragmatically inert. It is, for the most part, politically useless. What exactly is it that would constitute democratic action aside from deconstructing the commitments of any particular political action? What would the political task be, aside from showing how any particular political movement must not close in upon itself conceptually? This remains entirely unclear.

It is not that Derrida has nothing to say on the matter. For instance, in *Spectres of Marx* he cites the rise of what he calls the New International: those who, ignoring national borders, seek solidarity in confronting the oppressions of our time. These would be the participants in what was called the anti-globalization movement, the human rights workers aligned with NGOs, the union organizers who seek to remove unions from their traditional national alignments, etc. However, the activity of this New International, if that would be the name for it, is not well described as deconstructive. It is, instead, centered on the idea of the equality of anyone and everyone. It is animated by a spirit (to use Derrida's term) of solidarity that recognizes no classification and that acts as though democracy is to be created from below rather than imposed from above.

To put the point another way, the movements cited by Derrida as examples of democracy to come are better understood as examples of politics in Rancière's sense. They need not be read as deconstructive, and they do not clearly exhibit the complex aporetic structure that Derrida embraces as the character of democracy. Perhaps one can interpret them that way. It doesn't seem impossible to do so. However, to do so seems more an intellectual exercise than a political one. It foists a strange sort of messianism (what Derrida calls a messianism without messiah, since there is never a closure of the messianism) upon a set of movements that seem more concerned with solidarity across police orders. These movements are, simply put, exercises in creating democracy through acting on the presupposition of equality. To remain at the level of deconstruction is not to inform politics but to rise above it. It is to remain outside the fray rather than to engage it.

Rancière's approach to politics, then, cannot be assimilated to liberal theory, Habermas' theory, or into recent Derridean thinking about democracy. However, the approach itself, as we have described it, might be faced with an objection. It is an objection that, if it is right, returns us to traditional liberal theory. To see this objection, let's turn for a moment to the role equality plays in justifying a traditional distributive theory of justice. Consider John Rawls' justification of what he calls the difference principle. In Rawls' view, there are three fundamental principles of justice: the principle of equal liberty (roughly, a principle of noninterference), the principle of equal opportunity (again, roughly, a principle of nondiscrimination and perhaps affirmative opportunity), and the difference principle. The difference principle states that the worst off in a given social arrangement should be better off than they would be in any other arrangement. That is, those at the bottom should have a better level of existence than they would if the society they live in were arranged according to any other distributive pattern. So, if one were to pick a society in accordance with the difference principle, one would not care how well off one might be or how the middle class was doing. One would instead pick solely on the basis of how well the worst off were doing, relative to any other way the society could be arranged.

Rawls' justification for this principle involves an appeal to equality. Specifically, it appeals to the equality that structures the veil of ignorance, the method he uses for deriving principles of distributive justice. Behind the veil of ignorance, one does not know where one is going to find oneself in the society for which one is choosing principles. One has an equal chance of being anybody or anywhere: rich or poor, athletic or physically handicapped, religious or atheist, etc. Therefore, one must treat all possible social positions with equal respect. One must, in short, choose principles of distributive justice impartially. Roughly, the motivation for the difference principle is that those who have an equal chance of landing anywhere in a society will worry more about how badly off they can be rather than how well off, and will therefore choose to protect themselves from the effects of the worst possible scenario rather than take a chance on doing really well.

Rawls feels that in order to pick fair principles of distributive justice for a society, one must take all places one might wind up – that is, all the different places one might occupy in a society – into account. He uses the veil of ignorance to put people in a position (theoretically, at least) of taking all those places into account. And he believes that, if one thought reasonably about what principles one might choose for a society from the situation of the veil of ignorance, one would choose the principles of equal liberty, equal opportunity, and the difference principle.

Now who would be the object of this demonstration? Who might Rawls be trying to convince? In some philosophical sense, of course, he is trying to convince everyone of the justifiability of the principles, and particularly of the most controversial one: the difference principle. However, those at the bottom will hardly need convincing. It is those who are going to have to give something up, those who are the beneficiaries of a given social arrangement, that need to be convinced that redistributing some of their benefits is a just thing to do. The appeal to equality here serves not to address those at the bottom – or at least not fundamentally to address them – but instead to address those in the middle and particularly at the top.

We have already said that Rancière's view of equality does not address those in the middle or at the top; it addresses those at the bottom, those whose lives take place at the various wrong ends of social hierarchies. The presupposition of equality is not a distributive principle. It does not address those who either support or benefit from inequality. It does not constitute a justification for redress. In an important way, the presupposition of equality does not address those people at all, at least not directly. Rather, it is a call to those who struggle or who have reason to struggle, and a way to conceptualize the fundamental character of that struggle.

And here is where the problem seems to lie. The power of Rawls' appeal to equality (in the form of the method of the veil of ignorance) is that it offers a justification for redistributing social goods that addresses those who will have to suffer the redistribution. Those who will receive it do not need to be convinced. Rancière, on the other hand, does not address those at the top at all. He addresses precisely the people for whom justification is not needed: the people, the demos. This is not, it should be emphasized, to say that the people, the demos, the part that has no part, do not need a proof of their equality. Rancière is at pains to show that one of the most powerful aspects of the presupposition of equality is that it offers a proof to those presumed less than equal, a proof that arises from the character of their own political action. "This is the definition of a struggle for equality which can never be merely a demand upon the other, nor a pressure put upon him, but always simultaneously a proof given to oneself. This is what 'emancipation' means."[21]

A proof of this kind, however, is not the same thing as a justification of the type that Rawls' theory offers. Rancière's proof is a verification to oneself of one's own equality, and as a result is, as he says, emancipating. It emerges from one's own political action, and verifies, through the fact of action, one's own equality to those further up the social hierarchy. It does not offer a justification to those who do not benefit from the enacting of the presupposition.

Rawls' concept of equality, on the other hand, acts precisely to justify his principles to those who would not otherwise be inclined to be sympathetic toward them. At the risk of oversimplification, we might put the issue this way: while Rawls' appeal to the concept of equality acts as a justifier to those who need justification, Rancière, by placing equality as a presupposition for politics rather than as a distributive principle, can use equality as a justifier only to those who do not need justification. (They may need affirmation or verification of their equality, but they do not need justification for a loss they might suffer.) What, then, is the normative force of his concept of equality? Does it really perform the justificatory task that equality does for more traditional theories of justice? In other words, is the appeal to equality in Rancière's hands simply a call to the oppressed to exert their own equality, empty of any moral content relative to those against whom the oppressed struggle?

I believe that it does perform a task of justification, but in a very different way. It is true that the presupposition of equality does not appeal directly to those who are the beneficiaries of a given police order. This does not mean, however, that it does not affect them or that they do not have to face its justificatory power. To see why, consider what happens in a moment of politics, that is, a moment in which the demos is acting upon the presupposition of equality. As we have seen, to act politically in Rancière's sense is to create a dissensus. It is to refuse a given police order. This will not be without effect on those who are at the top of that order. They will be confronted with this presupposition, often in a very direct (if not very philosophical) way. To be confronted by a people acting out of the presupposition of equality is to have the police order one takes for granted challenged in the name of that equality. And the question that challenge raises is one of whether, indeed, one does believe in equality, whether one's response in the face of that challenge ratifies that presupposition or betrays one as a supporter of inequality.

In his book *On the Shores of Politics*, Rancière offers an example of how the presupposition of equality can work on those not involved in acting out the presupposition. He refers to a tailors' strike that occurs in the wake of the French charter of 1830, a charter that states the equality of every French citizen in its preamble. The strike seeks higher wages so that the tailors can live equally to their supervisors and owners. In discussing this example, Rancière offers a sort of syllogism: "the major premise contains what the law has to say; the minor, what is said or done elsewhere, any word or deed which contradicts the fundamental legal/political affirmation of equality."[22] What the strike accomplishes is to force the hand of both the master tailors and the legal authorities regarding the question of equality. They face a choice. Either they can ratify the presupposition of equality acted upon by the tailors or they can admit that they do not really believe in equality. As Rancière puts the point, "If Monsieur Persil [the French prosecutor] or Monsieur Schwartz [the head of the master tailors' association] is right to say what he says and do what he does, the preamble of the Charter must be deleted. It should read: the French people are not equal. If, by contrast, the major premiss is upheld, then Monsieur Persil or Monsieur Schwartz must speak or act differently."[23]

The presupposition of equality does, then, perform a similar role to that of Rawls' concept of equality. It does have a normative force, even upon those it does not directly address. It appeals to those who benefit from inequality, although it does so in a very different way from Rawls. Rawls appeals to equality as a method of convincing those who are better positioned that it is fair that they should be prepared to sacrifice some of what they have. Rancière's presupposition of equality works instead as a challenge. Moreover, it does so only in political situations. It does not have the hypothetical or abstract character of traditional liberal theories of equality. In other words, the presupposition of equality does not offer a justification of equality outside the contexts in which it is enacted. One cannot, as with Rawls, invoke the presupposition of equality outside of a given political context in order to justify a particular set of principles. Instead, the presupposition acts from within a situation of dissensus as a challenge to those who uphold a particular police order. This, of course, is in accordance with Rancière's conception of politics as something performed by the demos rather than distributed to them.

If we are to embrace Rancière's approach to politics, if we are to allot the honorific term *democracy* to it, we must ask what characterizes a democratic movement. Until now, we have offered a theoretical alternative to traditional views of democracy. In the rest of this book, will we look at particular struggles that exemplify democracy. But before we turn to them, let's linger briefly over the characteristics of democratic movements that accord with Rancière's view of equality. What does democracy in action, collective struggle that emerges out of the presupposition of equality, look like?

Let me approach these questions by isolating several elements of a democratic politics. These elements are not meant to be exhaustive, but they will give us a sense of what to look for when assessing whether a movement is democratic or asking how to go about forming or participating in one. There are five elements I would like to focus on. The initial two can be drawn directly from what has been said so far. First, a democratic politics is one that emerges from below rather than being granted from above. Second, a democratic politics is egalitarian in what might be called a *horizontal* sense. That is to say that those participating in it consider one another to be equal.

The next two elements have to do with the relation between those engaged in the politics and those who might be thought of as its adversaries. The third element is that a democratic politics must also be egalitarian in what might be called a *vertical* sense. Those against whom dissensus or resistance is to occur, those whom the police order places at the top, are also to be treated as equals. The fourth element, derived from the third one, is that a democratic politics must be oriented toward nonviolent action. There may be a place for violence, but that place can only be where there are no other alternatives and where the denial of equality is both egregious and steadfast.

The fifth element, which will involve returning to a Rancièrean term referred to quickly above – *le partage du sensible* – is that politics can happen anywhere, or almost anywhere. Although Rancière argues that politics happens rarely,[24] this is not because there are few places where it can happen. Rather, it is because it is so urgently discouraged. A democratic politics can emerge anywhere from the workplace to the classroom to the theater to the street.

The first element follows directly from Rancière's theoretical structure. A democratic politics is a creation of those who participate by acting together out of the presupposition of equality. As such, it is made rather than granted. Democracy comes to pass not where we receive it but where we produce it. This idea should be read alongside the oft-quoted pronouncement that freedom is not given, it is taken.

The second element refers to the formation of a community in the creation of a democratic politics. Rancière writes that, "Democracy is the community of sharing, in both senses of the term: a membership in a single world which can only be expressed in adversarial terms, and a coming together which can only occur in conflict."[25] To be engaged in a movement of political democracy is to be involved in a collective action, one that takes its members as equal participants in a struggle that is never solely a struggle *for* equality but, more important, out of its presupposition. This does not mean, of course, that everyone in a democratic politics must perform the same task, or that the struggle cannot also demand some form of equality. Regarding the former, there are those who may have expertise in some areas, and others who may have more time to give. However, in accordance with the presupposition of the equality of intelligence, expertise and time are contingent matters. They do not confer a special status upon those who possess them. Regarding the latter, the demand for some form of equality or recognition of equality can emerge out of the perceived disparity between how a demos has come to view itself (as equal) and how it is treated by others or by institutions in a particular society (as unequal). We will see several examples of that in this book.

The third and fourth elements are not discussed by Rancière. He posits dissensus at the heart of politics, but does not tell us how those who dissent are to treat those from whom they dissent. The proposal here is that we must extend the presupposition of equality not only to those who struggle but also to the elites who, willingly or unwillingly, wittingly or unwittingly, oppress them. The failure to do so is a failure of the presupposition of equality itself. The elites are not elite because of their superiority, to be sure. But neither are they elite because of their inferiority. Their actions must be resisted, as must the police order that benefits them. However, that resistance must recognize the equal humanity of those who see themselves as greater than equal to the rest of us.

This is why nonviolent action must be the default orientation of any democratic politics. We must be clear here. Nonviolent action is not passivity. It is a mistake to call it, as it has been called, passive resistance. On the contrary, most nonviolent action requires a greater degree of creative intervention than violence. To resist with weapons those who also possess weapons is an old story, and not a very interesting one. (We will see one case of resistance with weapons – the Zapatistas – but the interesting part of that resistance lies largely in what happens when the weapons are put down, or before they are even picked up.) To resist without weapons those who have them requires a greater reflection on one's resources and one's tactics. As we all know, there is a sad and tired history behind us of progressive movements gone bad because the resort to violence evolved from a strategy of resistance to a strategy of governing. It would be well to recognize that danger at the outset and keep, as best one can – and admittedly sometimes one cannot – an orientation toward nonviolent action.

The fifth element is that a democratic politics can be made almost anywhere. In order to see why, let me recall a term that Rancière has utilized increasingly in his recent writings: *le partage du sensible*, translated into English as *the partition* or *the distribution of the sensible*, although we should also keep in mind the French signification of *partage* also as sharing. As Rancière points out, the police order is not enforced simply by the police. It is also a matter of how the sensible is distributed, partitioned, and shared. Hierarchies are imposed by people's coming to see and experience their world in certain ways, ways that sustain and nourish those hierarchies. This is a point that has been historically documented by, among others, Michel Foucault. But if hierarchies are maintained at the level of the sensible, at the level of our experience of the world, so dissensus can operate there as well. Obviously, a politics of the kind envisioned by Rancière has nothing to do with politics in the electoral sense; that is nothing more than policing, and could not have less to do with democracy. Electoral politics has the same relation to democracy that watching a sporting event on television has to playing one. Politics happens on the ground, where we live. However, we live in so many arenas, from our family to our work to hobbies to our civic participation, and each of these arenas participates in a *partage du sensible*. (Whether there is a single *partage* that encompasses them all or several overlapping *partages* need not detain us here.) As we intervene politically on each of these, we can make them more democratic, disrupting the police order that maintains oppressive relationships in favor of a participation that starts from the idea that each participant is equal. From gender equality to workplace equality to equality in participation in athletic events, the presupposition of equality can operate everywhere there is a partition, distribution, and sharing of the sensible, that is to say, everywhere.

One might ask, in the face of these characteristics, whether such a politics is possible. What is the status of such a politics? Is it something that ever happens? Or is it an ideal against which we measure our actual political participation? How shall we think of it?

Surely there are in many cases of the more and the less when it comes to the question of whether a political intervention arises out of the presupposition of equality. How much, one might ask, is equality being presupposed in a given political movement? However, there are cases in which it appears so clearly as to be unmistakable. Let me cite briefly two here, just for an initial orientation, before we turn in depth to our case studies.

The historical case, one of which many readers will all be aware, is the series of lunch-counter sit-ins in the US during the civil rights movement. African Americans sat at lunch counters that were restricted to whites and tried to order lunch. It is hard to imagine a more crystalline example of acting collectively from the presupposition of equality. The message of the lunch-counter sit-ins was clear: those who sat down to order a meal presupposed themselves to be equal to those who were permitted to order meals. The violence that was visited upon them was nothing other than an attempt to prove otherwise, and attempt that backfired precisely because the nonviolence exhibited by the protestors maintained their sense of equality.

A more recent and smaller scale example of democratic politics is displayed in the movement that has come to be called Critical Mass. This is where folks with bicycles (and less often skateboards or roller skates) come together and collectively ride through the streets of a large city, slowing the automobile traffic and essentially turning streets into bike-friendly paths. Their motto is, "We are not blocking traffic; we are traffic." These rides are actions that presuppose the equal access to the streets of those who are involved in environmentally friendly forms of transportation with those who are not. As you can imagine, they have been met by a good deal of resistance from some motorists and city authorities, who are not yet ready to concede such a presupposed equality. The partition of the streets has long favored motorized traffic, the effects of global warming and environmental degradation notwithstanding.

There are other movements of democratic politics afoot as well. We will study five of them over the next four chapters, before turning to a more general reflection on the possibilities for democratic politics in our time. Each of the chapters will focus on a particular aspect of what we have discussed in this opening chapter. This is not because these movements themselves exemplify only one or another aspect of democratic action. Far from it. Each of these movements displays, to some degree, all of the central aspects of Rancière's depiction of democracy: the presupposition of equality, subjectification, dissensus from police identification. Rather, these studies will give us an opportunity to look more in depth at each of these aspects, while keeping the others in the background.

The next chapter will turn its attention to a little-known but very successful movement. This is the movement of refugees from the

Algerian civil war for citizenship in Montréal, Canada. It displays the idea of the presupposition of equality as clearly as the US civil rights movement of the 1960s did. The succeeding chapter discusses the first Palestinian intifada. There we will focus on the process of subjectification. The fourth chapter addresses the Zapastista movement in southern Mexico. This is the movement of indigenous peoples, particularly in Chiapas, who, particularly during the mid-1990s – although continuing today – resisted their marginalization by the Mexican state and especially its embrace of neoliberal economic policies. We will focus on Zapatismo as an advance over the identity politics that characterized much of the left in the US and elsewhere during the late 1980s and the 1990s. In this way, we can see the politics of equality as a refusal of the identities that are on offer in a particular police order.

The fifth chapter turns in a slightly different direction. Rancière has argued that one of the necessities of democracy is that it cannot be institutionalized.

> The community of equals can always be realized, but only on two conditions. First it is not a goal to be posited from the outset and endlessly reposited . . . The second condition, which is much like the first, may be expressed as follows: the community of equals can never achieve substantial form as a social institution. It is tied to the act of its own verification, which is forever in need of reiteration.[26]

In this passage, and elsewhere in his work, Rancière resists the idea that one can institutionalize or formalize a democratic movement. He is a bit ambiguous about the term institutionalization, and in particular whether it refers to particular social institutions or a whole society.

That chapter will test the question of whether one can institutionalize democracy, at least at the local level. We will discuss two long-standing democratic institutions: a food co-op near my home town of Clemson, South Carolina, and an anarchist publishing venture in Oakland, California. In both cases, we will find that, at least at the local level, it seems possible for some length of time to create institutions that function out of the presupposition of equality. We will not argue that it is possible (or that it is impossible) that an entire society can be so institutionalized. It seems unlikely, but we do not want to eliminate that possibility theoretically. In fact, as we will see, it would seem a betrayal of Rancière's larger political framework to insist in advance that a democratic politics cannot be institutionalized. This would make such a politics necessarily parasitic on the larger police order in which it takes place. However, one of the great strengths of his political view is that the presupposition of equality comes from the demos rather than that police order. A democratic politics, then, although it often begins in dissensus, need not end there. That, at least, is the argument of the penultimate chapter.

Is democracy possible in our time? Does it still work? The wager of this book, and the subject of its last chapter, is that it is possible, that it does work, if we look in the right place for it. It does not reside with those who proclaim to lead us, too often with our assent. And it does not reside in the preponderance of our current institutions, although they may at times allow for its appearance. Rather, it resides in us, in the decisions we take collectively to dissent from the police order that maintains itself everywhere around us. Democracy is up to us; it appears, when it does, out of our making. We must not then ask, as though from a distance, whether democracy still works. That is precisely the wrong question. We must ask instead – and it is a question that has never ceased to be our question – of whether we are up to creating it.

Notes

1 *The Political Thought of Jacques Rancière: Creating Equality*, Edinburgh and University Park: Edinburgh University Press and Penn State Press, 2008.
2 Sen, Amartya, *Inequality Reexamined*, Cambridge, MA: Harvard University Press, 1992, p. ix.
3 Rancière, Jacques, *Disagreement: Politics and Philosophy*, tr. Julie Rose, Minneapolis: University of Minnesota Press, 1999 (or. pub. 1995), p. 17.
4 See, especially, Rancière, Jaques, *La Leçon d'Althusser*, Paris: Gallimard, 1974.
5 For an excellent account of the events of May as well as its aftermath, see Kristin Ross' *May '68 and Its Afterlives*, Chicago: University of Chicago Press, 2002.
6 Much of this work is discussed in Rancière, Jacques, *The Nights of Labor: The Workers' Dream in Nineteenth-Century France*, tr. John Drury, Philadelphia: Temple University Press, 1989 (or. pub. 1981).
7 E.g. "Politics begins with a major wrong: the gap created by the empty freedom of the people and the arithmetical and geometrical order," *Disagreement*, p. 19.

8   Rancière, Jacques, *The Ignorant Schoolmaster: Five Lessons in Intellectual Emancipation*, tr. Kristin Ross, Palo Alto: Stanford University Press, 1991 (or. pub. 1987), p. 46.

9   *Disagreement*, p. 28.

10   *Disagreement*, p. 28.

11   Foucault, Michel, *Security, Territory, Population: Lectures at the Collège de France, 1977–78*, tr. Graham Burchell, New York: Palgrave Macmillan, 2007 (or. pub. 2004).

12   *Disagreement*, pp. 29–30.

13   *Disagreement*, p. 14.

14   Rancière, Jacques, *On the Shores of Politics*, tr. Liz Heron, London: Verso, 1995 (or. pub. 1990), pp. 32–3.

15   *Disagreement*, p. 35.

16   *Disagreement*, p. 37.

17   *Disagreement*, p. 59.

18   *The Ignorant Schoolmaster*, p. 72.

19   Rancière, Jacques, "Ten Theses on Politics," *Theory & Event*, vol. 5, no. 3, 2001.

20   Derrida, Jaques, *Rogues: Two Essays on Reason*, tr. Pascale-Anne Brault and Michael Nass, Palo Alto: Stanford University Press, 2005 (or. pub. 2002), p. 86.

21   *On the Shores of Politics*, p. 48.

22   *On the Shores of Politics*, p. 46.

23   *On the Shores of Politics*, p. 47.

24   "[P]olitics doesn't always happen – it actually happens very little or rarely," *Disagreement*, p. 17.

25   *On the Shores of Politics*, p. 49.

26   *On the Shores of Politics*, p. 84.

2

Equality among the Refugees:
Montréal's Sans-Statuts Algerian Movement

On May 12, 2002, three or four dozen people gathered in a small hall in Montréal. They heard several speakers discuss the recent years of their lives. One of those speakers was a young woman named Amel, who had three children. She had arrived in Montréal in 1999, during the height of the Algerian civil war. Like thousands of other Algerians, she had asked for refugee status. She explained to the gathering that, "I had two addresses in Blida, two of my children were born in Algiers. I lived in Blida but my passport was issued in Algiers. This sufficed to convince them [the immigration commission] to refuse me refugee status."[1] Another refugee, Ryad, had vowed never to leave Algeria, but finally did after he received five bullet wounds as he was leaving his house one day in Algeria. His crime was that of being the brother of someone who wrote pamphlets denouncing the Islamic fundamentalists. He had also been refused asylum, and therefore was among the thousand or so Algerians living in Montréal who had the status of sans-statut; that is, the status of no status.

Why were these people gathered here on this particular evening? The May 12 meeting was called in response to an announcement that, except for what happened after May 12, would have gone largely unnoticed among the Canadian people. A month earlier, on April 5, the Canadian minister of immigration, Denis Coderre, had lifted a moratorium on deporting Algerians refused asylum or immigrant status that had been in place since 1997. The original moratorium had itself been enacted in response to the continuing violence of Algeria's civil war, a violence that had eventually claimed the lives of over 150,000 Algerians.

The civil war had begun in 1992, when the first round of national election results indicated that the likely winner was the Islamic Salvation Front, the FIS. In order to understand how an Islamic party, one that turned out to be so brutal, could win a round of national elections, it is worth stepping back a bit, perhaps to 1962.

At that time, the National Liberation Front (FLN), the Algerian resistance movement, drove the French from Algeria. The resistance is immortalized in the film *The Battle of Algiers*. There are a couple of factors that have made the Algerian resistance movement particularly important. First, Algeria was France's central colonial stronghold in Africa. In fact, while other French colonies were exactly that – colonies – Algeria was considered part of France, even though the indigenous Algerians lived no better than those in officially colonized countries. Second, the Algerian resistance became a model of resistance for many other African countries seeking liberation from European colonialism. Because of its sustained, and ultimately successful, resistance to entrenched colonial rule, Algeria in general and the FLN in particular became emblematic of anti-colonial struggle, especially in Africa.

For most of the thirty years after its liberation from France, Algeria was a single-party state ruled by the FLN. This was not unusual in the Arab world, and indeed is not unusual today. However, the FLN was part of a secular Arab movement that went into decline with the failure of secular Arab unity in the Middle East. Although the story of this failure is a long one, and one whose legacy remains today, one might summarize it by saying that during the 1950s and 1960s the Arab world sought to unite against Western incursion and against Israel. Its failure on both fronts was perhaps ultimately signaled in 1978, when Egyptian President Anwar Sadat signed a peace treaty with Israeli Prime Minister Menachem Begin.

This failure is one of the reasons for the rise of Islamic fundamentalism. In some quarters, the secularism of Arab leaders was itself a legacy of European colonialism. Their inability to resist the West symbolized not only the West's political dominance but also the uselessness of resisting the West with its own secularism. Islam began to give people more of a sense of their identity than Arab unity (although, of course, this identity is itself fractured between Sunni and Shia, and at times along nationalist lines as well). In the meantime, Islamic organizations were working on the ground to offer social services to those who did not benefit from the secular policies of these Arab governments. That contrasted starkly with the corruption and authoritarian character of the secular regimes. Combined with the failure of those regimes, it helped lead to rise of Islamic fundamentalism in a number of Arab (and other Muslim) countries.

In Algeria, this rise was displayed forcefully on December 26, 1991, when the FIS won the first round of parliamentary elections. For many, voting for the FIS was a vote against the ruling party, which had lost its legitimacy not only through corruption but also because it was perceived as violently suppressing all dissent. This was exemplified by riots in 1988 which were violently suppressed by the government, but which led it to concede to demands for multi-party elections. It was these elections that led to the FIS victory.

In response to that victory, in January 1992 the army canceled the second round of elections, deposed President Chadli Bendjedid, outlawed all parties based on religion, and proceeded to govern without an electoral mandate. At that point, the FIS (and particularly a smaller, more violent splinter group – the Armed Islamic Movement) took up arms and began killing government officials, and then civilians, and eventually massacring whole villages. The government's response, if not equally brutal, was certainly brutal enough.[2] The war began to wane in 2002, but violence continued and it remained particularly dangerous for those who had fled to return, since they would be cloaked in suspicion to both the government (which has recently marginalized the Islamic resistance, partly through military defeat and partly through increased social services) and to the remnants of the Islamic resistance.

Caught in the middle of this civil war was the Berber population, descendants of the people who lived in Algeria before the arrival of Islam and the Arabic-speaking population. The Berbers, sometimes called Kabylians because of the region in Algeria where many of them are concentrated, were often targeted by both sides. Although they were not the subject of some of the most notorious massacres, they were often targeted because they were active in their own self-defense from early on in the civil war. They formed a large percentage of the refugees that came to Canada. In 1990, for instance, there were roughly 3,000 Algerians living in Québec. By 1996, when the civil war had been going on for four years, there were about 7,000, while by 2000 the number reached nearly 15,000.[3]

But why Canada? In her 2003 thesis Julie Mareschal, who studied the Berber refugee movement, explained that there were three reasons.[4] First, it was far away from Algeria. It seemed the civil war would not follow them there. Second, Montréal is francophone, and, since the French occupation, French has become the second language of Algeria. Finally, compared with France itself, it was easier to obtain refugee status in Canada. The upshot of all this is that during the Algerian civil war Canada was the favored country for Algerian refugees in general and Berber refugees in particular. Canada had responded to this influx with a protective measure in 1997 that permitted even those who had been refused asylum to remain in Canada. They had no papers, no formal status. In France they would be called the *sans-papiers*. In Canada, they were the *sans-statuts*, the difference being that the former often did not apply for papers, while the latter had applied for refugee status and were refused. Unlike the *sans-papiers*, they were entitled to limited access to health care, welfare, and a right to work; but they had no formal legal standing and were vulnerable to deportation at any time.

If the violence of the Algerian civil war remained, why was the moratorium on returning refused refugees lifted? A month before the lifting of the moratorium, Prime Minister Jean Chrétien had made a state visit to Algeria. He had been under pressure from Algerian President Abdelaziz Bouteflika to lift the moratorium, since it was an embarrassment to the Algerian state. Soon after Chrétien's return to Canada, immigration minister Coderre announced that the violence in Algeria had diminished and that it was safe for the *sans-statuts* to return. It is perhaps worth mentioning, at least in passing, that the following month, May 2002, the Canadian company SNC Lavalin, an engineering and construction giant, signed a contract with the Algerian government worth an estimated 141 million dollars. For reasons that may or may not have something to do with economics, then, the Canadian government was willing to return a thousand people to a war zone in which their lives would be at risk, especially since each of the refused, Amel and Riyad among them, would be marked for slaughter.

The story we have related so far is not an unfamiliar one. Countries deal with refugees and other potential immigrants on the basis of state self-interest rather than the stakes of those who seek refuge or work. The US has recently witnessed this with the debate on illegal immigration. In Paris, the 2005 riots called attention to the marginal status of North African immigrants in France. In Germany and England as well, enclaves of immigrants from Africa and Asia occupy the lower rungs of the social order, and provide fodder for elected politicians and religious leaders during difficult economic times. Those who are vulnerable, because they are vulnerable, are political pawns. And because they are vulnerable, they rarely act in solidarity with others, and rarely act publicly. It is often best, if one is alone and without protection, to install oneself within the social cracks rather than to confront openly the forces that oppress one. The latter course is usually an invitation to deportation.

It is what happened after the lifting of the moratorium on

deportation that gives the story of Montréal's Algerian *sans-statuts* its interest, both as a political lesson and as a philosophical one. It is a lesson that could be drawn from directly from the work of Jacques Rancière, whose work we canvassed in the previous chapter.

For Rancière, we can recall, politics concerns action that emerges from a framework of equality. Equality is not something that is distributed, and it is not something that people receive, as it is in traditional theories of justice. Equality, instead, is a *presupposition* of those who act on their own behalf. Otherwise put, people act, not in order to achieve equality, but out of the presupposition of their equality to others, and most often to those who consider them their inferiors. As Rancière puts the point: "Equality is not a given that politics then presses into service, an essence embodied in the law or a goal politics sets itself the task of attaining. It is a mere assumption that needs to be discerned within the practices implementing it."[5] That is to say, when people act in accordance with what Rancière calls *politics* and what I call a *democratic politics*, they can be "discerned" to be acting in according with the assumption of their own equality.

There is a subtle but important distinction Rancière is drawing here, one we did not discuss in the previous chapter, between those who act politically and those who are looking upon, analyzing, or describing such political action. The distinction is this. Those who are engaged in political action may not be telling themselves in so many words that they are acting out of the presupposition of their equality. They may not even use the term *equality* at all. During my interviews with several members and supporters of the movements of the *sans-statuts*, that particular word was not used. To be sure, no one avoided using it. It just didn't come up.

However, to act out of the presupposition of equality does not require that one use the word or any cognate word, just as to act out of fear does not require that one tell oneself that one is afraid or even be aware of one's own fear. It can, instead, be *discerned* as an animating assumption by those who are an audience for the movement, whether they are theorists or fellow activists or members of the population at large. What this quote of Rancière is pointing to is that in interpreting certain movements we may see the presupposition of equality at work, whether or not those involved in the movement themselves use the idea of equality overtly in thinking about or organizing their activities.

With this idea in hand, let's turn back to the movement of the *sans-statuts*. What happened in Montréal after the April 5 lifting of the moratorium on return? Some refugees, of course, fled the country or made arrangements for transfer to a third country. Some took their chances and accepted deportation back to Algeria. After all, the vulnerability of the *sans-statuts* gives them little or no leverage to negotiate with the government. Further, their isolation both politically and economically leaves them without resources to construct alternatives. However, most of them did not. The movement they formed, of which the May 12 meeting was an early example, was an attempt to call attention to their situation and the threat they faced. Moreover, the movement was not simply a plea. It was a demand for regularization of papers and an end to deportation. During my interviews with members of the movement, they were adamant that they were contributing members of Canadian society, and therefore deserved all the rights accorded to those who had Canadian papers. They pointed out that they came with education, skills, an ability to speak the language, and a desire to participate in the society in which they now found themselves. Nothing more could be asked of a citizen than that.[6]

If this were all, then the movement of the *sans-statuts* would be simply a demand for recognition, like many other movements of its kind. There was more, though. The movement was led by the *sans-statuts* themselves. Soon after April 5, the *Comité d'action des sans-statut*, or CASS, a group led largely by *sans-statuts*, issued three demands: the end of deportations of *sans-statuts*, the reinstatement of the moratorium, and the regularization of all *sans-statuts*. CASS was the centerpiece of the *sans-statut* movement. Formed in the spring of 2001 in the wake of the Canadian government's discussion of lifting the moratorium on returning Algerian refugees, CASS was directed and led by *sans-statuts*. While it received much support from other organizations, such as the Canadian No One is Illegal and, eventually, mainstream organizations like Amnesty International,[7] CASS remained an organization of *sans-statuts* and their supporters.

We must recognize the significance of this. At one level, we might say that the most vulnerable people of a society, those without any institutional support, engaged in an aggressive public campaign of meetings and demonstrations in order to press their case. In July, 2002, for instance, a hundred or so *sans-statuts* and sympathizers gathered outside Canada's Bureau of Immigration in order to demand an end to deportations. Later, on October 8, a larger demonstration in solidarity with a family who took refuge in a church (see below, the Bourouisa-Seddiki family) would draw hundreds of people. While it would be true to say that a vulnerable people without external support built a solidarity movement, putting matters this way would risk missing the central Rancièrean point. The members of CASS did not act like refugees. They did not hide. They did not accept their status as marginal. Although they were, quite literally, a part of Canadian society that had no part, they did not accept the state's refusal to give them a part. They acted out of the presupposition of their own equality. The public nature of their meetings and demonstrations were testimony to this. Although they had no status and no protection, and although they were under threat of imminent deportation, they acted as though none of this were true. In their demand for recognition, or, more specifically, for regularization, they acted as though they were already Canadian citizens who enjoyed all the rights those citizens took for granted. And, indeed, many Canadians stood alongside them as equals during their meetings and demonstrations.

Moreover, this action out of the presupposition of equality concerned not only their relation to Canadian society. It also concerned their relations to one another, and on two levels. First, within the immigrant community, there are hierarchical distinctions created by immigrant status. Essentially, these fall into three levels. At the top are the regularized immigrants themselves. These are the people who have left, but not fled, Algeria, and have become citizens through the slow process of assimilation. Second, there are the refugees. They may attain citizenship, but, unlike other immigrants, they have the stigma of having fled their society. They are also sometimes associated with terrorism, a commonplace in contemporary society. Finally, at the bottom, are the *sans-statuts*. Mareschal points out that, in contrast to immigrants and refugees, the *sans-statuts* "do not have the sense of liberation associated with refugees recognized by the Canadian state."[8] During the events of 2002, these distinctions, while not entirely effaced, began at least to be blurred. As CASS became more successful and garnered more attention, immigrants and refugees who had previously hesitated to be associated with the *sans-statuts* became more openly supportive.

Not only were class distinctions among the Algerian and particularly Kabylian immigrants blurred, so were the gender distinctions so central to traditional Arab and Berber culture. Although it would be too much to claim that men and women were entirely equal in CASS, there were women among the leadership and in the ranks of the movement. One woman I spoke with, a supporter of CASS although not herself a *sans-statut*, said that there was a tendency at big events to have mostly male speakers, but that there were several women central to CASS's informal leadership. Mareschal notes that, "In Algeria, the Imazighen [i.e. the Berbers] have a very particular mode of functioning. Horizontal and circular, traditional Berber organiza-tion is opposed to the vertical and linear model of the West."[9] Several of her interviewees invoked this mode of organization in reference to political organizing in Montréal. In Berber culture, however, the circle does not really include women. However, CASS, just as it blurred the class lines between immigrants, refugees, and *sans-statuts*, also blurred the lines, without entirely effacing them, regard-ing which gender was allowed inside the circle.

The political movement on behalf of and led by the *sans-statuts*, then, was a movement that, at least more or less, presupposed the equality of anyone and everyone. It presupposed that everyone is equally capable of creating a meaningful life alongside others, and it challenged the police order of the Canadian state in the name of that equality. As Rancière notes, "The essence of equality is not so much to unify as to declassify, to undo the supposed naturalness of orders and replace it with the controversial figures of division."[10] Moreover, the presupposition of equality was not simply a challenge leveled against those who were not Algerians; it was a presupposition that infiltrated the movement itself. Class and gender distinctions were effaced, leadership was informal, meetings allowed everyone a space to participate.

In order to underline the importance of this, we can turn away for a moment from the Algerian civil war to the Israeli occupation of Palestine, and in particular to the two intifadas of 1987 and 2000. The first intifada, which we will discuss in detail in the next chapter, was a popular uprising against the occupation. I had the opportunity to witness it first-hand, having gone on a human rights delegation to the occupied territories in 1988. What was remarkable at that time were the different levels of participation of the Palestinian population in the intifada. The Western media focused on the confrontations between young, male Palestinian stone-throwers and the US-backed advance weaponry of the Israeli army. Although the contrast here did capture accurately the balance of military strength between the Palestinians and the Israelis, it missed much of what was happening on the ground in Palestine.

The intifada was not simply a youth-led confrontation. It was an assertion of equality across and within Palestinian society. Our group visited "underground" educational centers where Palestinian children were being taught their own history, rather than the Israeli-sponsored history of standard schools that denied their history and their heritage. We saw a small pepper-processing plant that was run solely by women, who had decided that they should be involved at all levels of agricultural production, not just the picking of the peppers. We were given a tour of various small plots of land in Palestinian towns and cities, plots that were used to feed the local population when Israel imposed its many curfews on these towns. Essentially, during periods of curfew, when nobody was allowed out of their homes for days at a time (and were sometimes barred from standing in doorways or at their windows), at night people would surreptitiously pick vegetables from these plots and pass them from house to house.

Through these assertions of equality, both against the Israelis and within Palestinian society, a movement was created in which everyone had a stake and in which everyone participated. One of the reasons the first intifada lasted as long as it did – until the Oslo Accords of 1993 – was precisely that it engendered a sense of equality among the Palestinian people.

This is in sharp contrast to the second intifada. By 2000, Arafat's return to Palestine and his government's corrupt rule had destroyed the organizations created by the first intifada and centralized power in his government. Moreover, the introduction of weapons into the occupied territories created a sharp distinction between those who were engaged in resistance and those who were among the rest of the population. The latter became more of an audience to the intifada than a network of participants. It is not surprising, then, that the second intifada never took hold of the popular imagination of the Palestinians (nor the rest of the world) as the first one had. The second intifada was largely a violent resistance movement led by an armed avant-garde. Under those conditions, one could not act under the presupposition of equality, and for two reasons. First, violence against Israel, which was often indiscriminate, did not represent so much an action out of the presupposition of equality as a desperate war against another, far better armed, state. It would be difficult to discern the assumption of equality in the events of 2000 and after.

Second, and perhaps more important, the centralization of power and the introduction of weapons destroyed the presupposition of equality among those who resisted. It divided the population into a police order of participants and non-participants, combatants and spectators. It is no accident that the Islamic fundamentalist group Hamas, which was marginal during the first intifada, assumed such an important role during the second one. The presupposition of inequality (between believers and non-believers, between men and women) that is so much a part of Islamic fundamentalism (or, for that matter, any religious fundamentalism) found a home in the second intifada that it could never have found in the first.

It is perhaps worth pausing, in this contrast between the first and second intifadas, to consider the role violence plays in a democratic politics. It seems to me difficult, although perhaps not impossible, to retain the presupposition of equality in the presence of weapons. We will see in Chapter 4 the Zapatistas attempt to retain a democratic equality alongside a movement that, at least at some points, is largely a violent resistance. The success of the Zapatistas is not uncompromised by weapons. But it does stand out as an exception in the history of violent resistance. The introduction of weapons, and of violent resistance generally, has a tendency to militate against the presupposition of equality. Weapons tend to create hierarchies. And, once created, these hierarchies tend to be self-sustaining. One need only look at the history of anti-colonial resistance to recognize this.

This does not entail, and I don't want to claim, either that violent resistance cannot operate on the presupposition of equality or that all nonviolent resistance necessarily does. As for the former, the Zapatistas have made a valiant effort to keep the presupposition of equality alive. However, it has required an effort, precisely because of the tendency of weapons to introduce hierarchies. On the other side of the coin, nonviolence does not guarantee democracy. While the US civil rights movement had a strongly democratic character and did much to introduce the idea of the equality of African Americans, and in India the influence of Gandhi helped orient the resistance toward the presupposition of equality – especially of the "untouchables" – there is nothing about nonviolent resistance that bars the introduction of a hierarchical order. What I am pointing toward here are tendencies rather than inevitabilities.

What happened in the first Palestinian intifada, in contrast to the second one, was very much in keeping, although on a much larger scale, with the activities of CASS. By effacing distinctions of inequality both with the outside population (other Canadians in the case of CASS, the Israelis in the case of the Palestinians) and within their own ranks, both movements achieved a democratic politics that were able to mobilize large segments of previously politically marginal groups.

Rancière claims that one element of political action such as this is a process of what he calls *subjectification*. Let us recall his definition. "By subjectification I mean the production through a series of actions of a body and a capacity for enunciation not previously identifiable within a given field of experience, whose identification is thus part of the reconfiguration of a field of experience." Subjectification, which is the central focus of the next chapter, is the emergence of a particular *we* from a set of collective actions. Where there were once only disparate individuals, each struggling to survive and to keep from being deported, there emerged, under the name of CASS, a collective movement of *sans-statuts* who recognized themselves as part of a larger whole. Individual refugees began to experience themselves not so much as individuals, as outsiders whose job was to remain anonymous and without a past, but as part of a collective with a shared history and goals. This happened, not *in order* to create a political movement, but *through* the movement itself. Subjectification, we might say, was neither the basis for CASS nor its outcome. It was not the basis for CASS because there was no sense of collective solidarity that pre-existed its creation. It was not the outcome of CASS because the subjectification was experienced during the movement. In fact, in the post-movement period, people have mostly gone back to their lives. CASS itself was the subjectification; or better, since there were actors who were not in CASS but in solidarity with it, CASS was a central aspect of the subjectification of the movement of the *sans-statuts*. As Rancière has said, "Genuine participation is the invention of that unpredictable subject which momentarily occupies the street, the invention born of nothing but democracy itself."[11]

Moreover, as this collective politics took hold, those who were not a part of it began to recognize themselves in it. Not only Algerian immigrants, but other Canadian citizens began to see themselves mirrored in the *sans-statuts*, not as struggling refugees but as people seeking to create lives for themselves. One participant in the struggle told me, "Papers are papers. But we are human." That recognition, so often denied those who do not have the status of full citizenship, began to take hold as the struggle of the *sans-statuts* became more public in the months after Minister Coderre's April 5 declaration.

The reason for this has to do with a phrase in Rancière's passage. The subject that is produced by political action is one that is "not previously identifiable within a given field of experience, whose identification is thus part of the reconfiguration of a field of experience." That is to say that a subject appears, is produced, occupies a place in the social order that had previously not existed. We saw in the previous chapter that Rancière speaks of experience as involving a *partage du sensible*, a partition or division of the sensible. This *partage* is the creation of sensible elements in their relation to one another. Typically, the *partage du sensible* is an element of the police order. We perceive what we are taught to perceive in the ways we are taught to perceive it.

In order to see this, think of the way many whites perceive people of darker skin, or how Americans often perceive those who appear to be Hispanic. There is a threatening character to their existence, one that is not a matter of reasoning but is often an immediate reaction. The tendency of whites to cross a street, or at least to feel the urge, when people of darker skin are walking toward them at night, is a testimony to this. So is the immediate sense of superiority many men feel in the presence of women, a superiority that displays itself in a tendency to dominate discussion or to preen as though women formed some sort of audience. In fact, the *partage du sensible* can often lead to women's appearing invisible in the presence of men. Not literally, of course, but still perceptually; women are background objects rather than co-participants in a situation.

What a political movement can do, however, is to rearrange what and how we perceive, make us see something new or different, reconfigure the field of our experience. This is what happened in Québec during the middle months of 2002. Something appeared that had been previously invisible to much of Québécois society: the *sans-statuts*. Although "not previously identifiable," through CASS they become identifiable. And once identifiable, they could become identified with. First, they were visible, they were among us, they were no longer hidden. Then, as their visibility impressed itself upon Québécois society, they became, at least for some Québécois, part of us. The subjectification of the *sans-statuts* rearranged the *partage du sensible* of Québec's political world. (One interviewee suggested that this rearrangement touched on a deeper chord in Québec, where many Québécois feel that the larger Canadian state views them in much the same way they viewed the *sans-statuts*, as invisible elements of an anglophone country.)

For Rancière, it is movements like CASS and the Algerian refugees that constitute democracy. Extending an earlier citation from Rancière, "Democracy is the community of sharing, in both senses of the term: a membership in a single world which can only be expressed in adversarial terms, and a coming together which can only occur in conflict. To postulate a world of shared meaning is always transgressive."[12] Democracy, then, is a process, a process of political subjectification that is coextensive with the presupposition of equality and that transgresses the shared meanings, *le partage du sensible*, of a given police order.

But what of success? Isn't politics about change? And if so, doesn't its definition require that there be some sort of change in order for it to be a real political movement? In some sense, there is already change with the very appearance of the movement, a change in the partition or distribution of the sensible. If we go further than this, we risk betraying the character of democratic politics that Rancière has posited. For if we require political change in order for there to be a real politics, a democratic politics, then that politics depends not on the presupposition of equality but on the response of those who so often deny it. Politics becomes parasitic on those against whom it takes place, or upon the circumstances under which it takes place.

Political change is a product not only of those who engage in a political movement, but also of those whom they oppose and who oppose them, and of the circumstances in which the movement takes place. If the demos could create change solely through its own subjectification and activity, the world would be a very different place from the one it is now. In a way, in any democratic political movement of the type Rancière describes, the odds are stacked against change. This is because such a movement arises from below, among those who live at the wrong end of a hierarchy. It arises among the part that, in one way or another, has no part. Democratic political movements take place in resistance to a police order where many of the resources and much of the power[13] lie with those against whom they struggle. This does not mean that there are no resources on the side of those who resist. Often, the mere ability to refuse to cooperate with a police order constitutes a significant resource. (This resource is rarely utilized to its full potential, in part I think because in the *partage du sensible* of most police orders it is not visible to people as an option.) Nevertheless, one should not underestimate the obstacles a democratic movement faces.

Because of this, if one were to define a democratic politics on the basis of successful change, it would hold democracy hostage to those who would seek to deny it in the first place or to the peculiarities of the circumstances that militate against it. One would in effect be saying that a democratic movement is one that succeeds against anti-democratic forces. This would be an odd way to go about defining democracy. One of the virtues of Rancière's account of a democratic politics is precisely that it locates the existence or non-existence of democracy in the hands of those who struggle, rather than in those of the elites or the vagaries of the situation. In police orders that deny so much to so many, it returns to them and their activity the possibility of democracy.

This does not mean, however, that results are irrelevant. They matter. But they do not define a political movement. As Rancière puts it, a democratic politics "causes equality to have a real social effect, only when it mobilizes an *obligation* to hear."[14] A politics is democratic when its own character expresses the presupposition of equality. But it is successful when those in front of whom and against whom it takes place are forced to confront their own role in the police order. Did this happen with CASS? If Québécois society had its experience reconfigured, its *partage du sensible* rearranged, did the movement mobilize an obligation to hear among those in the Canadian state?

On October 20, 2002, six and a half months after the lifting of the moratorium on deportation, after a series of demonstrations and meetings with officials, a family of Algerian refugees facing deportation sought refuge in the United Union Church in Montréal. Mourad Bourouisa, his pregnant wife Yakout Seddiki, and their two-year-old son were scheduled to board a plane headed back to Algeria, but, fearing that they would be slaughtered upon their return, decided to ask for asylum in the church.[15] This proved to be the watershed event in the struggle of the *sans-statuts*. Although the Bourouisa-Seddiki family were not members of CASS, they were in contact with them, and received their support. The stand-off lasted ten days, and on October 30, the Canadian federal and Québécois government agreed to a new procedure for reviewing the files of the *sans-statuts*. Henceforth, those who had been denied papers by the Canadian authorities could apply to have their situation re-evaluated separately through a Québécois procedure. Thus, the thousand Algerian *sans-statuts* would have available to them a means of being accepted as refugees, and eventually Canadian citizens.

Under this new procedure, many of the *sans-statuts* became legal. CASS's activities changed somewhat, focusing not only on advocacy but also on helping people file the proper documents in the new review procedure. However, not everyone was covered. For instance, I interviewed a man who had long been refused under the new procedure because he could not prove that he had actually been a *sans-statut* under the old rules. Although his situation was being regularized, it had taken years of legal wrangling to do so. In the meantime, he lived in fear of being deported back to Algeria, and could not engage in building a life in Canada. The most famous among those who were refused, however, is the case of Mohammed Cherfi, one of the leaders of CASS. The Canadian government decided to deport him, saying that he had not "integrated" himself into Canadian society, although, I was told, he was a French teacher. The problem, CASS members told me, was that his militancy on behalf of the *sans-statuts* was thought to be a threat to the Canadian government. He also took refuge in a church, but in March, 2004, he was taken from the church and deported to the US, where, ironically, he received refugee status in 2005. As of this writing, he is still trying to return to Canada.[16]

The struggle, then, continued past the October 2002 accord, although gradually at a diminished level as people began to be regularized. Perhaps the most public event was a sit-in in Minister Coderre's office in May 2003, where eleven *sans-statuts* and two sympathizers were beaten and tasered by the police. They were eventually brought to trial, and, particularly in light of the brutal treatment they received, acquitted on a technicality of all charges in February 2006.

Rancière writes that, "A community of equals is an insubstantial community of individuals engaged in the ongoing creation of equality. Anything else paraded under this banner is either a trick, a school or a military unit."[17] The movement of the *sans-statuts* was, and to a lesser extent continues to be, the creation of precisely such an insubstantial community. Built on nothing other than the presupposition of their equality to one another and to those in whose midst they found themselves, they organized a campaign that, in the end, mobilized an obligation to hear. Whether or not such a community must remain "insubstantial," that is, without an institutional character, is a question we will return to in Chapter 5, when we ask whether a democratic movement can become institutionalized. What must be recognized, however, is the part that has no part in a society can, at least sometimes, and in the times in which we live, create a part for themselves, impose themselves as having a part. Or, as Rancière would have it, in the face of the police orders that govern us, politics remains among our possibilities, when and where there is the context and the will to create it.

In the next chapter, we turn to the question of subjectification, which, we have seen, is a central aspect of a democratic politics. The emergence of subjectification is not only part of what must take place in order for a democratic movement to happen; the strength of subjectification can be an indicator of the strength, the depth, and the longevity of a movement.

Notes

I would like to thank all those who took the time to interview with me about the *sans-statuts* movement, and especially Mabrouk Rabahi, who generously set up discussions, translated when it was needed, commented helpfully on an earlier draft of this paper, and generally played the part of the perfect host. In addition to the members of CASS who discussed the organization and the movement with me, I would also like to thank Julie Mareschal and Andréa Schmidt for both interviewing and offering valuable suggestions on an earlier draft of this paper.

1 *Alfa*, no. 46, May, 2002, p. 13. All translations from the French are mine.
2 There are a number of histories of the Algerian civil war. One of the most comprehensive, *The Algerian Civil War, 1990–1998*, was written under the pseudonym of Luis Martinez (New York: Columbia University Press, 2000, or. pub. 1998). His particular thesis, that the war was a product of a military *imaginaire* directed at the social advancement of the actors in the struggle, has affinities with the social theories of Pierre Bourdieu. That point is beyond our concerns here.
3 Mareschal, Julie, "Orienter et réinventer ses pratiques citoyennes: le cas des immigrants et réfugiés Kabyles á Montréal," *Diversité urbaine*, vol. 4, no. 1, spring 2004, p. 93.
4 Mareschal, Julie, "Pratiques citoyennes des immigrants et réfugiés kabyles à Montréal," Québec: Université Laval, 2003.
5 *Disagreement*, p. 33.
6 Mareschal confirms this in her thesis. See esp., ch. 5.
7 Mareschal, Julie, "Politiques répressives et droits des réfugies: vers de nouvelles formes de solidarités," *Vivre Ensemble*, vol. 12, no. 42, summer, 2004, p. 6.
8 Mareschal, "Pratiques citoyennes," p. 107.
9 Mareschal, "Pratiques citoyennes," p. 85.
10 *On the Shores of Politics*, pp. 32–3.
11 *On the Shores of Politics*, p. 61.
12 *On the Shores of Politics*, p. 49.
13 I use the term *power* here in an everyday sense. I should note that I have spent many years thinking about and writing on the concept of power

as it appears in the work of Michel Foucault. That is a very different notion of power, much more sophisticated than the way I am using it here. What I'm getting at here is something closer to what Foucault calls *juridical power*.

14 *On the Shores of Politics*, p. 86.
15 www.cbc.ca/canada/story/2002/10/21/algerians_021021.html.
16 For more on Cherfi's case, see Mareschal's "Politiques répressives et droits des réfugies: vers de nouvelles formes de solidarités."
17 *On the Shores of Politics*, p. 84.

3

Subjectification in the First Palestinian Intifada

For those who have been involved in progressive struggle, there is very little more exciting than to watch an egalitarian movement grow. One can see it on people's faces. Listlessness and despair give way to hope and a sense of direction. Solidarity replaces gossip and pettiness. People begin to believe in themselves and in one another, not merely to survive but to thrive. The future takes on a new meaning. Involvement in the struggle allows one to see these changes from the inside, even if one is not necessarily a "member" of the struggling group. Although I was not witness to nor involved in the struggle of the Algerian refugees in Montréal, when I later interviewed people involved in the movement I could sense its aftereffects. The several people I spoke with sensed that there was a life now available for them that there would not have been without the movement. And they recognized that it was together, in collective action, that they had achieved the availability of that life.

One of the elements that Rancière describes as central to a democratic politics is subjectification. We saw in Chapter 1 that he defines subjectification this way: "By subjectification I mean the production through a series of actions of a body and a capacity for enunciation not previously identifiable within a given field of experience, whose identification is thus part of the reconfiguration of the field of experience."[1] Subjectification is not only an ineliminable moment of a politics of equality. In some struggles, it may be the most important moment. Because egalitarian struggles are created by those who are marginalized in a society, those who have been denied social and often material resources (as well as those in solidarity with them), they often fail or at best succeed only partially. Rancière also notes, as we saw, that an egalitarian movement "causes equality to have a real social effect, only when it mobilizes an *obligation* to hear."[2]

Creating the obligation to hear is difficult. In the case we will focus on here, there is a particular deafness at work that, at the moment of this writing, seems unlikely to be cured any time soon. However, as Rancière argues, the existence of a democratic politics does not rely on creating that obligation. It is not how those in power respond that defines the existence of a democratic politics. It is how those at the wrong end of a social hierarchy act and think of themselves that determine whether a politics of equality is in play. In that determination, the emergence of subjectification is central.

Before watching subjectification at work, we should understand a little better what Rancière is getting at when he invokes the term. It involves the production of something through a series of actions and enunciations. The something that is produced was, in some way, not there before, or at least not identifiable before. Finally, that something that is produced that was not identifiable before reconfigures the field of experience. We can take each of these elements in turn and say something general about them before turning to the first Palestinian intifada, where we can see them at work.

The something that is produced through a series of actions and enunciations is precisely a collective subject. Before political action, there is no *we* who is acting. There are only individuals going about their business. Occasionally there are individuals who criticize the police order of things. More often there are people who rebel against their situation in uncoordinated and often self-serving ways. Crime, for instance, is often a symptom of marginalization. As Rancière says, outside of a democratic politics "there is only the order of domination or the disorder of revolt."[3] The order of domination is the police order at work. It keeps the hierarchy intact. The disorder of revolt pushes against the police order, but not in the way of equality or of social change. It consists in individual resistance, either in a rational way for the sake of that individual or in an irrational way out of desperation or despair. Neither of these constitutes a democratic politics, although sometimes the latter is, because of a misplaced romanticism, confused with such a politics. A riot, for instance, is not an exercise of democratic politics. It is, instead, symptomatic of the need for one.

A subjectification emerges when a *we* comes to be as a result of the coordinated actions and enunciations of a group of people. If a riot is not an example of subjectification, strikes or demonstrations often are. In a strike, for instance, workers who are isolated from or even pitted against one another come together in a collective whole. They act and they speak as a whole, as members of a collective. This collective is not simply a psychological one. The collectivity is not only in people's heads. That is why Rancière emphasizes actions and enunciations. It is through doing, not simply through thinking, that subjecification is produced. This does not mean that thinking plays no role in subjectification. Thinking is required in order to produce the right actions and enunciations. Also, people in the midst of a democratic politics think differently about themselves and their world. For instance, they think in terms of their future more and differently from the way they had before. But, just as thinking one is in love does not make a love relationship, thinking of oneself in solidarity with others does not create a subjectification. It is the product of doings and sayings.

The second part of the definition states that the something that is produced was not previously identifiable in the field of experience. The *we* that emerges through sayings and doings did not, in some sense, exist before those sayings and doings. This may seem to be an odd thing to claim. Certainly there were, say, women before the suffragist movement. There were African Americans before the civil rights movement. Moreover, women and African Americans were identifiable within the field of social experience previous to their movements (although, in the US, African Americans were identified as Negroes). In what sense were they not previously identifiable?

One example Rancière uses to illustrate subjectification is the trial of the revolutionary Auguste Blanqui in 1832. When Blanqui was asked his profession, he replied that he was a proletarian. The magistrate challenges this reply, denying that proletarian is the name of a profession. Blanqui counters, "It is the profession of thirty million Frenchmen who live off their labor and who are deprived of political rights."[4] The term *proletarian*, as a term of subjectification, refers to something more than a group of people. It refers to a movement of people that may have been identified previous to the movement as individuals, but are now identified as a group, as a *we*. There were women as individuals before the suffragist movement, but during that movement there were women as, if we can put it this way, *women-equal-to-men*. There were workers before there were worker's movements (and, of course, there were worker's movements before Blanqui), but there were *proletarians* only when there were workers as a movement of equality.

As we mentioned briefly in Chapter 1, and will see in detail in the next, the *we* that arises out of a subjectification is not the *we* of identity politics. There is a similarity between the two, in that both are group formations in solidarity. However, the character of the group in identity politics is very different from that of a group in a democratic politics of equality. Rancière marks this difference when he says that

> A political subject is not a group that "becomes aware" of itself, finds its voice, imposes its weight on society. It is an operator that connects and disconnects different areas, regions, identities, functions, and capacities existing in the configuration of a given experience – that is, in the nexus of distributions of the police order and whatever equality is already inscribed there, however fragile and fleeting such inscriptions may be.[5]

In this passage the key contrast is between a group's becoming aware of itself and imposing its voice, on the one hand, and connecting and disconnecting in the name of equality, on the other. Identity politics focuses on the former, democratic politics on the latter.

A democratic politics does not seek the identity of a group. It creates what one might call an identity, but that identity – that *we* – does not have any particular borders, even when it assumes a name that seems to imply it, for example women or gays or proletarians. The element that binds together the individuals in a democratic group, whatever it calls itself, is not identity but equality. In that sense, in a democratic politics the name of the collective subject, the term by which the subjectification goes, is simply a placeholder. It is an important placeholder, since it responds to the particular context in which it arises. It challenges a particular hierarchy at a particular site in a particular police order. The gay rights movement, for instance, could not reasonably be called the Burma rights movement, since it is struggling against the presupposed inequality of gays, not Burmese. However, what is of moment in that movement that calls itself the gay rights movement is not gayness, but equality. In that sense, then, the name of a subjectification is not the name of a group that becomes aware of itself, but of a group that is created through a variety of people's connections to one another and disconnections from previous stereotypes in order to proceed in sayings and doings under the banner of equality.

It is precisely that type of group that is not previously identifiable in the field of experience. As we saw in Chapter 1, Rancière uses the term *partage du sensible*, partition or division of the sensible, to indicate that in a police order there is a certain arrangement of perception that reinforces hierarchical orders. The appearance of a collective subject – or, perhaps better, since Rancière often insists on politics as a process, the emergence of a subjectification – disrupts that particular perception. The something that appears – women-equal-to-men, gays-equal-to-straights, Palestinians-equal-to-Israelis – was not there before. And, when it does appear, it reconfigures the *partage*. This is the third element of the definition of subjectification. To reconfigure the field of experience is to make things appear differently from the way they did before. That is what a democratic politics accomplishes.

We can see this reconfiguration at the simplest level as simply the appearance of something new. A field of experience is reconfigured when a new object is added to it. In this case, the new object is the subjectification. But things go deeper than that. If women present themselves as equal to men (often alongside men who are also part of the subjectification), then women will appear differently in the field of experience. Their perceived passivity, obedience, or lack of intelligence – these will drop away as part of the way they appear. In their stead will emerge activity, insistence, and intelligence, perhaps alongside a sense of threat to the sensible field itself. This new character of the field of experience will appear to men, to be sure. But it will likely also appear to women. Women will begin not only to think of themselves differently, but also begin to appear differently to themselves. The perceptual experience of both men and women will change. It will be reconfigured to take on the changes that the subjectification has created.

Often, this is what is most disruptive about a subjectification. Its existence challenges the perceptual order, the *partage du sensible*, of the police order. It is disorienting to have one's perceptual categories reconfigured, and many people will resist it, particularly those who are not among the demos in question. For example, to *see* immigrants as equal to oneself – not merely to believe it in an abstract way, but to have it color one's perceptual experience – is not very easy, and not very comfortable, for people who have come to view their national fellows as a privileged group. This is perhaps one of the sources of the violent resistance that movements of equality often meet.

The particular subjectification we will follow in this chapter is that of the Palestinian rights movement during the first intifada, which started in December 1987. The most commonly cited ending of the first intifada is the Oslo Accords of 1993. However, the intifada was largely disrupted during the first Gulf War in 1990. We will focus here on the early years of the intifada, from 1987 to 1989. What is particularly enlightening about focusing on the first intifada is not only that it is a striking example of subjectification. It also allows us to contrast that intifada with the second intifada, which started in 2000. The latter, I will argue, is not a subjectification in Rancière's sense, because it does not operate from the presupposition of equality, either within its ranks or in relation to Israel. Comparing the two intifadas, as we began to do in the previous chapter, will allow us then to see more clearly what it means to be a collective subject or a process of subjectification as part of a democratic politics.

The first Palestinian intifada (which means *awakening* or *shaking off* in Arabic) began in on December 8, 1987. Its origins lie much earlier, though, in the Israeli occupation of Palestine. There is much to say about this history; all that can be offered here are some important facts that will have to serve as background.[6] In May 1948, Israel declared itself a state. That declaration was immediately followed by a war in which Israel gained 80 percent of what had been Palestine under the British Mandate that dated back to the end of World War I. However, before the outbreak of the war, Israel had driven hundreds of thousands of Palestinians from their homes. At the cessation of hostilities, roughly 700,000 Palestinians had been displaced.

Between 1948 and 1967, most of the Palestinians who remained in what was Mandatory Palestine under the British occupied two non-contiguous areas of land: the Gaza Strip and the West Bank. The Gaza Strip was administered by Egypt and the West Bank by Jordan. Then, in the wake of the war of 1967, Israel captured both areas of land (in addition to the Golan Heights in Syria). It immediately began to allow Israeli settlers to occupy this land.[7] This is in violation of international law, which stipulates that one cannot settle one's own population on territory belonging to the occupied people. (Nor can one take people from occupied territory into one's own territory, which Israel routinely does when it arrests Palestinians.) By the time of the second intifada of 2000, Israel had nearly 200,000 settlers in the occupied territories, the great majority of them in the West Bank.

The Israeli occupation of the West Bank and Gaza Strip has been egregious. Not only have settlers been allowed to move in and Palestinians imprisoned in Israel. Large tracts of Palestinian land have been confiscated and its inhabitants turned into day laborers for Israeli firms. Checkpoints have been set up outside of towns and villages that have impeded traffic and commerce and provided places where Israeli soldiers routinely harass Palestinians. All attempts at self-governance have been met with brutal repression, as have all forms of resistance against the occupation (where, for instance, Israeli soldiers have not hesitated to shoot at children demonstrators).

Palestinians have been demonized by the Israeli leadership, referred to as roaches and vermin and, in the case of Israeli Prime Minister Golda Meir, had their very existence as a people denied. As one resident of the West Bank explained to me when I visited Palestine during the first intifada in 1988, under the Jordanians everyone was allowed to live as they liked as long as they didn't engage in politics. Under the occupation, however, there was an active attempt to destroy their way of life.

There had, of course, been resistance to the occupation. The Palestine Liberation Organization (PLO), which originally formed in 1964, staged raids against Israel. In 1972, a radical wing of the PLO killed eleven Israeli soldiers at the Munich Olympics. There were other actions as well, some of them terrorist, others not. What there had not been was a general popular uprising against the occupation. There are many reasons for this. Perhaps most important, Palestinian society, dating back to before 1948, was rural and feudal in structure. It did not possess a cohesive national identity of the kind that characterizes most industrial societies, including that of Israel. Also, there were rifts within the leadership of that society, among the privileged landowners as well as between landowners and the religious leadership. Finally, since 1967 the Israeli occupation made coordination and communication difficult. It built a road structure that bypassed Palestinian towns and villages in favor of Israeli settlements, and generally attempted to disrupt Palestinian political activity. And, as a side effect of Israel's land confiscation, Palestinians who had previously been farmers were turned into itinerant workers for Israel. Their reliance on Israel for jobs, then, made solidarity among them difficult.

To everyone except many of the Palestinians themselves, then, what happened in reaction to the events on December 8, 1987, was quite a surprise. On that day, an Israeli military vehicle crashed into a truck that was carrying Palestinian workers from their day jobs in Israel. Four Palestinians were killed and others injured.[8] In itself, this event was not unusual. Israeli forces routinely killed Palestinians, sometimes by accident, other times not. Moreover, in reaction to previous killings, Palestinians often protested, particularly at the funerals of the slaughtered. Predictably, the protests would subside after a few days. What distinguished the protests after these funerals was that they didn't stop. They started in the Jabaliya refugee camp, which later proudly called itself the heart of the intifada, and then spread across Gaza and then the West Bank.

What most Westerners saw of the intifada was the clash of stone-throwing youth – the *shabab* – and Israeli military forces. The images of these clashes were fodder for television. I witnessed the preparation for one of these confrontations from a rooftop in the West Bank. What would often happen was that young Palestinian men with kefiyahs across their faces (to prevent identification and to help protect against the effects of tear gas) would block certain passageways through their villages by erecting barricades. This forced Israeli patrol vehicles to take alternative routes, often through narrower streets. There they would be met by other shabab throwing stones at the soldiers and their vehicles. In the narrower streets, with hidden alleyways, it was difficult to fire on the stone-throwers. Moreover, retreat for the vehicles was also difficult, since it required a maneuver to reverse through a small, often winding passage.

One might think that, even given the tactical advantages the Palestinians arranged for themselves this way, they would still be at a major military disadvantage. After all, Israel has one of the most advanced militaries in the world, supplied not only by their own massive military budget but by the United States as well. How could stones tossed by hand, or at best sling-shot, successfully battle against such an army? In a sense, they could not. From December 1987 through December 1993, the Israeli human rights organization Be'tselem reports 1,095 Palestinians killed by the Israeli army; by contrast, around 100 Israelis were killed between December 1987 and December 1992.[9] Looked at this way, the intifada could be seen as a military failure.

However, this would miss the true character of this aspect of the intifada. The salient character of the confrontations lay not in military victory or loss but in two other areas: the dynamic of non-violent resistance, and the empowerment and subjectification of the Palestinian people. These two areas will turn out to overlap. The first, the dynamic of nonviolent resistance, is described by Gene Sharp in the third volume of his three-volume *The Politics of Nonviolent Action*. He calls this aspect of the dynamic political *jiu-jitsu*.[10] It is a way of getting the more oppressive and more powerful side to have the assertion of its power backfire against it. By provoking or goading the oppressor into overreacting against resistance to its power, sympathy is gained for the struggle both within and outside the oppressed population. Within the oppressed population, people who had not been previously active are mobilized. They see what is happening to their fellow members and are themselves moved to engage in resistance. Outside the oppressed population, third parties begin to recognize more clearly the oppression that is being suffered. They see what had been hidden from them before: that there is violence and oppression being directed against a people. In short, this dynamic strengthens internal opposition while garnering external support.

Technically, the throwing of stones is not a form of nonviolent resistance. We will see below forms of resistance that are clearly nonviolent. However, given the massive Israeli military response, the dynamic they set in motion is the same. People who saw the images of advanced weaponry being directed against stone-throwers recognized the disproportion of power that was in play. Furthermore, Israel contributed to this dynamic as the Palestinian uprising refused to subside. Early in the intifada, Israeli Defense Minister (later Prime Minister) Yitzhak Rabin announced a policy of "force, might, and beatings" would be applied to Palestinian protestors. Scenes of the enactment of that policy were also shown on television, displaying not only the imbalance of power against the Palestinians but also the way in which that imbalance was used in oppressive ways. Television viewers around the world were treated to displays of groups of Israeli soldiers mercilessly beating unarmed Palestinians.

The other area where these confrontations lent their force was to the participants themselves. Although militarily *over*powered, the stone-throwers began to see themselves as politically *em*powered. They were cheered on by other Palestinians, but more important, they became actors in a coordinated effort to resist the occupation. One woman described for me the feeling of exhilaration in throwing a stone. (Although most of the stone-throwers were men, there were women involved as well.) She said it made her feel as though she had some real power against the occupation. Of course, throwing a stone is not a major display of power, and she recognized this. The sense of power came from somewhere else. It stemmed from her participation in a collective movement of resistance. And, in participating, at least two changes occurred for her. First, she moved from being passive to being active, not in general (she was an activist before the intifada), but directly in the face of the power confronting her. Second, she asserted her equality to those who were oppressing her. They could fight her, indeed, and maybe even defeat her. But she, in her turn, could stand up to them face to face.

The empowerment of Palestinians by their stone-throwing youth is particularly relevant to their presupposition of equality. In Chapter

1, I argued that a democratic politics is oriented toward, even if not fully embracing of, nonviolent resistance. Here we can see why. The Palestinians were labeled by Israel as terrorists. Of course, there were – and are – terrorists among the Palestinians. One might point out the irony of Israel's labeling Palestinians as terrorists when its own policy involves the ongoing systematic terrorizing of an entire population. But the point at issue here concerns the Palestinians. To assert oneself against an army through throwing stones is, among other things, to expose oneself without hiding behind advanced armor. The message here is something like this: we as a people can face your tanks and your helicopters and your high-speed bullets. We, then, are equal to you. This, I believe, was a powerful element of the confrontations with Israel in the Palestinian townships.

Alongside the presupposition of equality, and inseparable from it, is the emergence of a *we*, of a subjectification. The stone-throwers formed coordinated groups. They supported one another and acted with solidarity against a common threat. Rancière writes, "Genuine participation is the invention of that unpredictable subject which momentarily occupies the street, the invention of a movement born of nothing but democracy itself . . . The test of democracy must ever be in democracy's own image: versatile, sporadic – and founded on trust."[11] It is difficult to image a more apt summation of the activity of the stone-throwers, right down to the momentary occupation of the street. In trusting one another within the context of a collective action presupposing equality, the stone-throwers formed a collective subject, or, to use the more active term Rancière invokes, they engaged in a subjectification.

We should be clear here that these confrontations with the Israeli army in Palestinian neighborhoods were not the product solely of spontaneous decision or local initiative. Early into the intifada, there emerged a Unified National Leadership (UNL or, as it was sometimes called, UNLU – Unified National Leadership of the Uprising). When I was in Palestine in September 1988, it was also called the Underground National Leadership, since its leaflets were composed in secret and distributed clandestinely throughout the occupied territories. The UNL was composed of people in Palestine who were involved in the local committees, not the official Palestinian leadership, which, with its leader Yasser Arafat, was in exile in Tunis. Moreover, as Don Peretz, early chronicler of the first intifada points out, it was the UNL and not the exiled leadership that organized, inasmuch as it could, the confrontations. Moreover, the decisions of the UNL were the result of a participatory process. "Given the grass-roots origins of the UNLU, it is not surprising that its decisions are the result of a democratic process, made unanimously after consultation with local committees and at times with the PLO [i.e. the exiled leadership]."[12] It was the UNL that, on January 14, 1988, issued what were called the Fourteen Demands that oriented the goals of the intifada for the next couple of years. These demands included the ending of human rights abuses against the Palestinians as well as the lifting of restrictions on political activity, the cessation of settlements, the release of political prisoners, and the termination of economic exploitation.[13]

One might wonder whether the direction offered by the UNL undercut the egalitarian character of the intifada. Was there a hierarchy created by the UNL that formed at least the outlines of what Rancière calls a police order? This seems to me a mistaken interpretation, for several reasons. First, as mentioned, the decisions and operation of the UNL reflected events at the local level. Second, people's participation in the confrontations and strikes called for by the UNL was voluntary. The UNL had no real authority over anyone; participation was chosen by the participants. Although there was an atmosphere that oriented individual Palestinians toward participation in the intifada, and to that extent a particular *partage du sensible* that affected them, this *partage* was not the result of UNL directives, but of the momentum of the intifada itself. Finally, there is no contradiction between egalitarianism on the one hand and some degree of centralized coordination on the other. There is certainly a *danger* of centralized coordination becoming an authority removed from the demos. But it does not have to be that way. Coordination can be one of the tasks that the demos has called for or would call for. Without coordination, it becomes difficult to sustain a movement or to orient it strategically. Coordination can be something everyone agrees to even if everyone is not participating in it. (In Chapter 5, we will investigate a local food co-op that operates precisely on this model.) The UNL seemed more or less to operate in that way. It helped bring together various activities and demands that were arising from the Palestinian demos, and give them expression in a way that not only reflected those demands but also allowed for strategic coordination across the population.

The demonstrations and stone-throwing were only the most visible manifestations of the first intifada. There were numerous other activities, and only some of them involved protesting the occupation. For instance, there were strike days, where Palestinians shop owners, particularly in tourist areas, would close their shops early or not open them at all. This would educate tourists about the intifada at the same time that it protested Israeli policies. Perhaps the most interesting activities, however, particularly from the viewpoint of subjectification, were those that did not have a public face. I will briefly canvass three of the ones that I saw when I was in Palestine.

One of these was a consequence of the demonstrations; it was a local medical clinic in a refugee camp in Gaza. At that time, there was little in the way of available medical facilities, especially in the refugee camps. (The refugee camps contain those Palestinians – and their descendants – who were forced off their land in 1948 or in 1967. The conditions in those camps was, and remains, significantly worse than that of the Palestinians who already lived in Gaza and the West Bank before 1948 or 1967.) The United Nations Relief and Works Agency (UNRWA), which oversees much of the medical care in Gaza, was overwhelmed financially and could not provide adequate medical care. It also provided such care only at the discretion of Israel, who had fired the previous UNRWA director for being too forceful about the need for medical facilities for the Palestinians in Gaza. At this time, because of the Israeli response to demonstrations, there were many more wounded Palestinians than there would normally be. Moreover, Israel used high-speed military bullets in the guns they fired at Palestinian demonstrators. These bullets were not only capable of penetrating light military armor; they also had a tight spin, so when they entered the body they would careen around, breaking and sometimes shattering various bones near their point of entry.

One of the projects of the local popular committees that arose before and during the intifada was to fund and staff a medical clinic in the Jabaliya refugee camp. This clinic, which was primitive by most Western standards, had several functions. First, it treated injuries resulting from demonstrations. Second, it provided general medical care. Third, it provided cheap dental care, which wasn't available elsewhere. This was an important function, since many of the Israeli beatings of demonstrators were aimed at the head and mouth. Fourth, it educated the local populace about first aid techniques. Fifth, it would send doctors out at night during curfews. Israel would often place curfews on the refugee camps, not allowing anyone outside their homes. At times the army would use these curfews as opportunities to enter the homes of suspected resisters and beat them and their family members, since the curfew would prevent the appearance of witnesses. The locally funded doctors would follow-up and treat these people as best they could in their homes, or would try to arrange clandestine transportation to the clinic.

The operation of such a clinic, primitive as it was, required two different types of sacrifice. The first was financial. Gaza is an extremely poor area. When I was there, it was sometimes called the largest prison camp in the world, and conditions have worsened considerably since then. Unemployment in Gaza is currently around 45 percent.[14] The Jabalya refugee camp is the most crowded camp in Gaza, known both for its stark conditions and its history of resistance to the occupation. Funding for a medical clinic is bound to put a strain on the meager financial resources of the camp's population. And yet people contributed enough to sustain the clinic. The other type of sacrifice was borne by those who worked in the clinic. The doctors and other medical staff put in long hours with limited medical resources under conditions made tense by the occupation and surrounding demonstrations. And yet doctors, nurses, and others participated.

We might be tempted merely to admire these sacrifices. But that would miss their political point. Things were not always like this in Gaza. During the several weeks I was in Palestine, I was told several times that before the intifada, people generally tended to their own business. Solidarity was absent. What the intifada brought out, of which this clinic was an example, was the participation in collective projects in and through which people formed a sense of a *we*. One does not give of one's time and risk arrest or beatings unless one feels that the point of that time and risk is worth the concession. The concessions made by the clinic's staff and funders were for the sake of their fellow camp residents, residents with whom they felt more in common after the commencement of the intifada than before it.

The other two activities centrally involved the participation of women. The fact of women's participation is significant, particularly in a conservative culture where women were often denied autonomy. (And, with the rise of Islamic fundamentalism in the second intifada, women are once again facing obstacles they thought they had overcome with the first intifada.) We will see the importance of women's struggles within a resistance movement again in the next chapter on the Zapatistas. There, what came to be called "the revolution within the revolution" forced the emergence of women as leaders in a movement with an indigenous base that was not traditionally oriented toward women's equality. In much the same way, the first intifada, while it did not introduce the ideas of women's participation and leadership, hastened their development. Peretz notes that,

> Women have played an increasingly prominent role in Palestinian society during recent decades, a development that was greatly accelerated by the Intifada. With thousands of men in prisons in far larger numbers than ever before, a vacuum was created in many sectors of the community that women began to fill. Not only did they assume leadership roles in political and communal organizations and in the popular committees, but they began to challenge the traditional economic division of labor.[15]

In asking the question of whether a resistance movement is really characterized by the presupposition of equality, one way to address that question is to look at the role of women. Where women's participation, institutions, and leadership begin to show themselves, particularly in resistance movements in more traditional communities and societies, there is evidence that the presupposition of equality is beginning to take hold. In the first intifada, this evidence was prominently on display.

One of the activities women were particularly involved in was the creation of early education centers. These centers were often illegal, since Israel sought to control the education of Palestinians. The struggle over knowledge is often an important one, as the historical studies of Michel Foucault remind us, since it determines the sense of who one is. In schools monitored by Israel, Palestinian history and culture were either neglected or denied. (Later, when I gave talks on Palestine, I was also struck at how skewed a view many Israelis who attended those talks had of their own history. This is particularly surprising since Israel's press is remarkably open – far more so than, say, the US press – and over the past twenty-five years several prominent Israeli historians have been vigilant in exposing the dark underside of official Israeli history.) What these centers provided was a Palestinian-oriented education, one that emphasized Palestinian history and experience. Clearly, these centers formed a threat to Israel, since (I was told) five of them had already been closed over the course of the intifada.

The other activity, of which I saw one example, was the rise of women's cooperatives. The one I visited was in a small Palestinian village on the West Bank. There were few jobs for women there, since most of the work was agricultural, and those jobs were largely taken by

men. So the women decided to form a women's agricultural cooperative. They produced and packaged cucumber, eggplant, jam, olives, and
peppers (I should note for the record that the latter were hot peppers –
very hot peppers). It was a small outfit – fourteen women, two storage
rooms. But the women explained that this type of production allowed
them a sense of empowerment and economic self-sufficiency. It also
disrupted the village's traditional gender relationships.

This particular cooperative was started in 1986, a year or so
before the intifada. They started selling in July, 1987, five months
before the intifada's outbreak. This should not be surprising, and it
helps explain the intifada itself. The intifada could not have been an
entirely spontaneous uprising. If it were composed solely of street
demonstrations, perhaps it could have been. But it wasn't. Aside
from the medical facilities, the alternative educational and day-care
centers, and the women's cooperatives, there were other activities as
well. These were coordinated by the local popular committees, of
which there were many before the intifada began. Ze'ev Schiff and
Ehud Ya'ari, Israeli journalists and authors of *Intifada: The Inside
Story of the Palestinian Uprising that Changed the Middle East
Equation*, point out that there were popular committees for agricul-
ture, for judicial disputes, for land allocation, and for health, as well
as for active resistance. "No one knows," they write, "just how many
popular committees existed in the territories, but there must have
been hundreds of them . . . The striking feature of the popular committees was their lack of uniformity, as befits a grassroots operation
. . . People who had always kept their distance from the PLO's institutions plunged into committee work with relish, despite the risk of
being punished for their pains."[16]

Schiff and Ya'ari claim that the popular committees were largely a
result of the intifada's outbreak. This seems unlikely on the face of it,
given the immediate coordination that the intifada displayed. In addition, there seemed to be evidence, for example the women's cooperative I visited, that much of the infrastructure for the intifada was in
place before December 1987. During my time in Palestine, one of our
guides, who was centrally involved in the uprising, claimed that the
local popular committees predated the intifada, but that the events of
December 8 catalyzed them into a movement of mass civil resistance.
Before that, he said, the committees were organizing and waiting for
a precipitant moment. The outrage and demonstrations during and
after the funerals for the four Palestinian workers convinced many of
them that the time had come for a popular uprising. They began then

to coordinate more seriously and to intersect with various spontaneous resistance groups, especially the stone-throwing youth. My own guess is that this explanation is largely right, although it was clear, as Schiff and Ya'ari point out, that as the intifada gained momentum, there was a much greater degree of participation on local popular committees than there had been before the end of 1987.

We should note, not only in passing but because it will prove important for the second intifada of 2000, that the movement on the ground during the first intifada was not a seamless one. First, there were tensions between the local popular committees and UNL on the one hand and the official Palestinian leadership in exile in Tunis on the other. Although the UNL was in contact with the official leadership, they did not take orders from them. The first intifada was dominantly a bottom-up movement. The UNL was a center of coordination, but, as we have seen, it was responsive to the local popular committees and composed of members from those committees. The second tension was more marginal during the first intifada but would prove fateful later. That was the tension between the UNL and local popular committees on the one hand and Hamas on the other.

Hamas is the main Islamic resistance organization in Palestine. It arose from the Muslim Brotherhood, and cast itself as the Islamic alternative to the PLO and the UNL. In August 1988, it issued its own covenant as a counter to the PLO charter and the demands formulated through the UNL.[17] Later, Israeli officials admitted giving support to Hamas during its early campaigns in order to split the Palestinian movement. When I was there, Palestinians, particularly those in the West Bank, openly suspected as much. They pointed out that during strike days called by the UNL Israeli soldiers would beat people and sometimes force shop owners to open their stores, while nothing like this would happen when Hamas called for strikes. At that time, and continuing today, Hamas is stronger in Gaza than in the West Bank, since Gaza is more religiously oriented than the West Bank. At the time of this writing, Hamas forces control Gaza, and Hamas won a majority of seats in the Palestinian parliament in 2006.

During the first intifada, Hamas was a far weaker player than it has been during the second intifada, for reasons we will return to below. Particularly on the West Bank, the tenets of Islamic fundamentalism – denying women's equality, refusing solidarity with Christian Palestinians (about 10 percent of Palestine's population), imposing a strict religious hierarchy – ran counter to the egalitarian orientation of the first intifada's participants.

The first Palestinian intifada offers one of the great recent examples of subjectification as Rancière envisions it. The first element of subjectification, as we saw, is the formation of a collective subject through action. The action we have recounted was that of the emergence of a collective subject. We can see this in several ways. A number of people I spoke with in Palestine described the disparate character of the Palestinian population before the intifada. As a rural and agriculturally based society, the Palestinian collectivity was not oriented toward mass, coordinated resistance. This is not to say that there had been no Palestinian resistance to the occupation between 1967 and 1987. There had been. But this resistance had not reached across the divisions among Palestinians in order to form a unified front. The traditional divisions between men and women and between rich and poor were not the only divisions in play. There were the divisions between those in refugee camps and those in villages, and even between the refugees from 1948 and those from 1967 (the land belonging to the former lay in Israel, whereas the land belonging to the latter remained in the occupied territories). The effect of these divisions was to prevent the kind of solidarity that could form the basis for meaningful resistance.

Of course, Israeli policies had a central role to play in eliciting mass resistance. Recall that for Palestinians, particularly those on the West Bank, Jordanian rule between 1949 and 1967 was far less egregious than the Israeli occupation would prove to be. Several residents of the West Bank told me that as long as they avoided politics, they were allowed to go about their business. They did not have their land confiscated, their villages isolated by bypass roads, and their people turned into day laborers. However, the existence of oppression does not automatically cause resistance. There has to be movement from the side of the oppressed. In the case of Palestine, that movement had to come from the kind of struggle that would bind these separate sub-populations together into a whole. The whole was precisely the subjectification, the integration of groups through collective and coordinated action that, to one degree or another, presupposed the equality of all participants.

This coordination was not entirely spontaneous. We noted that there were a number of groups pre-existing the intifada that paved the way for its emergence. They did not, and could not, ignite the spark that would set it off. They could only prepare the ground so that when an event took place, as it did on December 8, 1987, that would ignite that spark, they could take advantage of it to keep the embers burning. Because of this, Rancière's view that subjectification and a democratic politics co-emerge is precisely correct. Subjectification does not precede such a politics, although conditions that foster subjectification might. The *we* that arises within a democratic politics does not exist entirely pre-formed and then only subsequently engage in collective action. Among oppressed people, there is generally too much division (often actively promoted by oppressors) and too much desperation for that. Instead, more often there are organizers or militants or small organizations that are at work seeking to create solidarity with only limited success. The politics that emerges brings far larger groups into solidarity because of its active character and because the presupposition of equality animating it runs directly counter to the hierarchical order under which they have been living.

Conversely, a democratic politics does not entirely precede subjectification. Subjectification is not a spontaneous outgrowth of a democratic politics. It grows alongside and within such a politics. If subjectification were to emerge only after the expression of a democratic politics, that politics would not be a politics of the *we*, of a *collective* of equals. It is difficult to imagine a politics arising on such a ground, or better such a non-ground. In order for a democratic politics to take hold and to move beyond blind revolt, there has to be a coordinated aspect to it. This requires people working together in a collective way. If this collective way of working is not going to be one of avant-gardist politics with a clear distinction between leaders and followers, then its basis must lie in the collective presupposition of the equality of participants. But, of course, this coordinated action by a collective animated by the presupposition of one another's equality has been given a name by Rancière: subjectification.

Subjectification does not display only the emergence of a collective subject. That collective subject is, in Rancière's definition of subjectification, a rearrangement of the partition or division of the sensible through the identification of something that had previously been invisible. Before the intifada, the Palestinians had not been entirely invisible, either to the Israelis or to the world. But they were not visible as a Palestinian people, and especially as a demos. Perhaps this is most trenchantly summed up in the words of Prime Minister Golda Meier in 1969, "There is no such thing as a Palestinian people." This was intended as a denial of Palestinian aspirations for statehood. It was at the same time, however, a denial of a collective subject.

In the period before December 1987, it would not have been difficult for non-Palestinians to deny the existence of such a subject.

First, whatever resistance existed seemed, at least in media accounts, to stem from Palestinian terrorism. This itself had two effects: it delegitimized the Palestinian experience and it made it easy to stereotype the Palestinian people. I do not want to deny here that Palestinians who committed terrorist acts were complicit in all this. They were. There was (and remains) a complex structure of Israeli claims of victimization, media passivity and at times collusion, and Palestinian terrorism. The latter reinforces the former two. In any case, to the degree that such a thing as a Palestinian existed within the *partage* of the world scene, it was as something less than fully civilized and certainly not as a member of a people.

In addition, particularly for Israelis, it was possible before the first intifada to ignore or suppress knowledge of the Palestinian experience most of the time. Israeli policy toward those it occupied made separation between Israelis and Palestinians the normal run of things. The Green Line, which runs across the 1949 armistice line in Jerusalem, was rarely crossed by Israelis except those in military uniform. Roads in the occupied territories were built to circumvent Palestinian towns and villages. Palestinian workers in Israel were largely invisible to Israelis, much as lower-class workers are invisible to middle- and upper-class people the world over.[18] For an Israeli, the occupation before the intifada was largely something that was far away, and thus easy to deny to oneself. The exception to this, of course, would be military service in the occupied territories, which did involve a lot of Israelis. However, once out of uniform, Israelis had both the motivation and the opportunity to deny what they saw in Palestine.

The intifada changed all this. Not only were Palestinians visible in a way they hadn't been before, filling television screens the world over. More pointedly, they were visible in a particular way, as *Palestinian people resisting an occupation*. Palestinians appeared as a demos, a demos that was not merely a victim and not merely a terrorist (recall Rancière's quote that without a democratic politics "there is only the order of domination or the disorder of revolt"). Instead, they appeared as a people, standing together to resist something egregious. The stone-throwers pitting themselves against tanks and helicopters offered particularly eloquent images of this. The willingness of young people to risk their lives in a radically unequal military confrontation bespoke their desire, and made people who saw them (and, for the first months of the intifada, nobody with a TV could avoid seeing them) sympathize with their situation in a way that had been previously unthinkable, because that situation literally did not appear to them. The first intifada made something appear that was "not previously identifiable within a given field of experience."

And, indeed, this appearance rearranged the *partage* of both Israelis and others. Israelis, in particular, had to confront a perception of themselves as something other than what they had previously perceived. Before the first intifada, their view of themselves was one of a people under siege, fighting for their survival. That is a difficult view to retain when the images one sees of one's fellows is of soldiers using advanced military weaponry against a civilian population in struggle against its occupation. In a complementary fashion, Israeli perceptions of Palestinians changed, in ways we have just detailed. As a result of this, the partition of the sensible presented a different texture, because the place of Israelis and of Palestinians in that partition began to change. When one experiences oneself as an oppressor rather than a victim, one's entire experience – right down to one's perceptual experience – begins to falter. Things don't look the same as they did before. One's fellows are no longer exactly one's comrades. The world takes on an accusatory aspect that it did not possess before. One looks in the mirror and does not, perhaps, see exactly the same person one used to see.

What was true for many Israelis was also true for others around the world, although in a less concentrated way. And it was also true for the Palestinians themselves. Although numerous Palestinians had prepared for something like the intifada, its strength and sustainability surprised many Palestinians themselves. As the intifada progressed, Palestinians began to see themselves and their world differently. An image of their passivity was replaced with an image of their activity. Hope rather than despair infused their lives and brightened their perceptual world. As the Israeli *partage* changed, so did the Palestinian *partage*. We saw in Chapter 1 Rancière's claim that, "This is the definition of a struggle for equality which can never be merely a demand upon the other, nor a pressure put upon him, but always simultaneously a proof given to oneself. This is what 'emancipation' means." The first intifada was an emancipation for many Palestinians. It brought them a sense of empowerment. With empowerment comes an alteration in one's perception of the world. The sensible is partitioned and divided differently. Spaces and people that appeared threatening are no longer so. The world presents fewer obstacles and more opportunity. In this way, just as the Israeli *partage* changed by having the Palestinian *people* appear to them, so the Palestinian *partage* changed once they began to appear to themselves more clearly as a people.

The concept of an Israeli *partage* and a Palestinian *partage* is, of course, oversimplified. As we saw in Chapter 1, there is no single division between those who have a part and those who do not. And so there cannot be simply two separate ways of dividing or partitioning the sensible. Moreover, a *partage* can be shared between oppressor and oppressed. One of the reasons people allow themselves to remain oppressed is that they share a way of perceiving the world in common with those who oppress them; for example, many oppressed people perceive the world in terms of their own inferiority. Finally, the division of the sensible is not reducible to the police order. Although a police order plays a significant role in the arrangement of one's sensible world, that world is not simply a product of the police order. It is a product of the various aspects of one's life: one's friends, one's loves, one's genetic orientation, etc.

To speak of an Israeli and a Palestinian *partage du sensible*, then, is to paint in broad brushstrokes what is really a more nuanced picture. What I would like to capture with this distinction is not what all Israelis perceive or what all Palestinians perceive, but rather what one perceives from the standpoint of an Israeli or a Palestinian as such, especially vis-à-vis their relationship to each other. For many Israelis, Palestinians did not, and still do not, appear in their world except in times of violence and then only as a personal threat. For many Palestinians, Israelis appeared in their world constantly, but as an overwhelming and irresistible force. These partitions of the sensible changed with the first intifada. It is certainly true that not all perception is reducible to the hierarchical orders of the police or the emancipatory character of resistance. But neither can we deny that perception is colored by them. It is that coloration we have been exploring here.

One of the consequences of the first intifada was the 1993 Oslo Accords, a set of agreements about the framework for peace between Israel and Palestine. Although an analysis of the Oslo Accords would take us far afield, we should isolate two changes that occurred in Palestine after the Accords, one that would help provoke the second intifada and one that would change its character. The first was Israel's increasing dispossession of Palestinian land. As historian Ilan Pappe notes, "Massive land confiscation and settlement expansion marked the four years (1992–6) of the Labour premiership . . . by 1996 the settler population had increased by 48 percent in the West Bank and 62 percent in the Gaza Strip."[19] This dispossession had two contradictory effects. It placed the Palestinian population in an increasingly precarious position while at the same time making the possibility of resolving the occupation more remote. The more Israeli settlers inhabited Palestinian land, the more difficult it would be to remove them. The border between Palestine and Israel became increasingly blurred, which subverted the possibility of a two-state solution to the occupation.

The other change was the return of Yasser Arafat and the PLO to the occupied territories. This, at it turns out, was a disaster for the Palestinians. The return of the PLO afforded Palestinians the possibility of electing their own officials (although, under the Israeli occupation, elected officials are not the same thing as a government). However, once in power, the PLO proceeded to crush the grassroots political organizations that had been the backbone of the intifada. What had once been a vibrant democratic movement became, with the return of the official Palestinian leadership, a population subservient to a corrupt hierarchy.[20]

These two changes alone do not suffice for explaining the second Palestinian intifada. The first, however, goes a good distance toward explaining its initial motivation, while the second helps explain its course. For the purposes of this chapter, it is the course of the second intifada, in contrast to that of the first, that is of interest.

The second or al-Aksa intifada began in October of 2000. Its precipitant was a visit by Ariel Sharon, a terrorist against Palestinians for fifty years and soon to be Prime Minister of Israel, to the al-Aqsa mosque near the Temple Mount and the Dome of the Rock in the Old City of Jerusalem. Previous to this visit were the failed Camp David negotiations between Prime Minister Ehud Barak and Yasser Arafat. The visit was followed by Palestinian demonstrations that were brutally suppressed by the Israeli army, and then by armed conflict between Israel and the Palestinians. At the time of this writing, the conflict remains, although Palestinian resistance has ebbed.[21] However, the character of the second intifada was far different from that of the first one. In particular, the second intifada was not a mass uprising. It involved more military confrontation, and far fewer people were actively involved. The reasons for this shed light on the character of a democratic politics.

The situation previous to the second intifada was very different from the first one. There are five related differences we can point to. First and most important is the existence of governing institutions in the occupied territories. These governing institutions, in particular the Palestinian Authority, were not the equivalent of a government. They did not control their borders or their airspace. They could not grant passports. And the area they controlled was not universally recognized as a state. However, while during the first intifada whatever governing of the population occurred happened through local popular committees, before the second intifada it happened through the Palestinian Authority and its related institutions.

The Palestinian Authority, in turn, dismantled the local popular committees. This is the second difference. Under its governance, on-the-ground organizing was discouraged, and resistance to the Authority often met with prison and human rights abuses. Yasser Arafat was never fond of challenges to his authority, and did not tolerate them during his tenure as Palestinian Authority President. As a result, the self-governance of Palestinian society became hierarchical rather than egalitarian.

A third difference, related to these first two, is the existence of light arms in Palestine. Although the Palestinian Authority had no military, it did have an armed police force. When hostilities broke out with Israel, this police force saw itself in military terms struggling against Israel. Of course, given the strength of the Israeli military, their arms did them little good. The major contribution of Palestinian light weapons to the struggle against the Israeli military was in giving Israel a public justification for its various incursions into and attacks upon the Palestinian population. The effect it had among the Palestinians was, as we saw in the previous chapter, to divide the population between those who were armed and those who were not. This division reinforced the hierarchy within the Palestinian population, and consequently prevented the formation of a subjectification among Palestinians. And, as we noted in the first chapter, violence tends toward hierarchy and against equality. Since subjectification is founded on equality, the result of having a police force in occupied Palestine when the second intifada broke out was to separate the population largely into two groups: resisters with weapons and non-resisters without weapons. (There were exceptions to this, of course, but this was the general run of things.) This, combined with the fact that the Palestinian Authority had dismantled the local popular committees and either co-opted or marginalized their leadership, created a form of resistance that was avant-gardist and hierarchical rather than participatory and egalitarian.

The fourth difference concerned the rise of Islamic fundamentalism throughout the Arab world. Hamas, which had initially been covertly supported by Israel as a counterweight to the PLO and secular Palestinian resistance, was now part of a larger Islamic resistance network. It had gained strength particularly in the Gaza Strip. And, since Islamic fundamentalism, like all religious fundamentalisms, is inegalitarian in orientation, it divided the Palestinian population into those who resist – men – and those who support resistance – women. This development ended much of the progress women had made as a result of their activities during the first intifada. In addition, because of the anti-Semitic orientation of Hamas, its inegalitarian view of Jews contributed to a hierarchical perspective on the world and to the kind of violence that results from such a hierarchy. (We should emphasize, however, that the violence resulting from Hamas' racist inegalitarianism pales in comparison with that of Israel's racist inega-litarianism toward the Palestinians. On this point, Hamas, which sees itself as countering Israeli policy, actually mirrors it.)

The final difference arose as a result of Israeli policy. Although Israel agreed as part of the Oslo Accords not to expand settlements, they continued to appropriate Palestinian land and to put settlers on that land. In fact, settlement activity during the Oslo period (1993–2000) occurred at a *faster* pace than it had previously. According to Be'tselem, the number of settlers in the occupied territories at the time of the Accords was 116,000.[22] (That would reflect settlement activity for the twenty-six years between 1967 and 1993.) By the beginning of the second intifada, seven years later, it was 194,000. Moreover, Israel set up a vast system of checkpoints throughout the territories where they harassed Palestinians and made economic movement difficult. By the time of the second intifada, Palestinians were worse off economically than they had been before the signing of the Oslo Accords. This, combined with the other differences, contributed to a sense of desolation that preceded the second intifada and that was not characteristic of the conditions in 1987.

The second intifada, then, was hierarchical, violent, and non-participatory. As a result of this, it did not succeed in forming a subjectification of the kind that characterized the first intifada. There are at least two lessons to be drawn from this. One is in accordance with what we claimed in Chapter 1. Violence does not promote either egalitarianism or subjectification. It divides the demos rather than uniting it. This does not mean that violence is never justified among an oppressed population. There are times when it is the only viable alternative. What it does mean is that there is always a cost to violence, and that where violence is employed that cost must be taken into account, and countered to the extent possible. Countering violence is difficult, if for no other reason than the fact that some people have guns while others do not. However, this situation must be recognized for what it is rather than avoided if hierarchy is not simply to repeat itself, one police order to replace a previous one.

The other lesson is that internal hierarchy itself prevents subjectification. By internal hierarchy I mean a hierarchy or police order within the demos. Where some have authority over others, it is difficult to form a *we*. Any *we* that is formed will likely be subtended by an *us* and a *them*. As Rancière points out, subjectification is inseparable from a democratic politics. Where one is lacking, the other will go wanting as well. The second intifada is a negative lesson in how this happens. Its contrast on this point with the first intifada could not be more stark. Subjectification is co-extensive with the existence of people acting collectively out of the presupposition of their equality. Introducing inequality into political resistance destroys the movement of subjectification. It is possible, of course, to form a political subject of some sort within the parameters of a hierarchical resistance movement. But that subject will be an impoverished one. It will not have the solidarity and dynamism of a subjectification, which co-emerges with a fully democratic politics. Among the lessons to be learned from comparing the first and second intifadas, this stands out as a central one, one that can and should inform both theoretical understandings of and activist engagements in democratic political movements in the contemporary world.

Notes

1 *Disagreement*, p. 35.
2 *On the Shores of Politics*, p. 86.
3 *Disagreement*, p. 12.
4 Quoted in *Disagreement*, p. 37.
5 *Disagreement*, p. 40.
6 There are many accounts of the history of Israel and Palestine. One recent overview of the entire history offered by a progressive Israeli historian is *A History of Modern Palestine* by Ilan Pappe (Cambridge: Cambridge University Press, 2004). Perhaps the most ground-breaking history from the Israeli "revisionist" historians, historians who have challenged the heroic myths of Israel's founding, is Benny Morris' *The Birth of the Palestinian Refugee Problem, 1947–1949* (Cambridge: Cambridge University Press, 1987). Morris has moved well to the right since this history appeared, although he stands by this history as an accurate one. An excellent, if dated, history of US relations with Israel is Stephen Green's *Taking Sides: America's Secret Relations with a Militant Israel*, Brattleboro: Amana Books, 1988.

7   For an account of Israeli settlement activity preceding the first intifada, see Geoffrey Aronson's *Creating Facts: Israel, Palestinians, and the West Bank*, Washington, DC: Institute for Palestine Studies, 1987.

8   Of the histories of the intifada, one of the best is an early one, Don Peretz's *Intifada: The Palestinian Uprising*, Boulder: Westview Press, 1990. Although published while the intifada was still in full swing, it gives an excellent overview of the events and their immediate impact.

9   Morris, Benny, *Righteous Victims: A History of the Zionist–Arab Conflict 1881–2001*. New York: Random House, 2001, p. 596.

10 Sharp, Gene, *The Politics of Nonviolent Action, Part 3: The Dynamics of Nonviolent Action*, Boston: Porter Sargent, 1973.

11 *On the Shores of Politics*, p. 61.

12 Peretz, *Intifada*, p. 89.

13 A translation of the full text of the Fourteen Demands is in Peretz, *Intifada*, pp. 201–3.

14 *Ha'aretz* (an Israeli daily Newspaper) reporting a UNRWA figure on July 28, 2008, http://www.haaretz.com/hasen/spages/1006282.html

15 Peretz, *Intifada*, p. 96.

16 Schiff, Ze'ev and Ya'ari, Ehud, *Intifada: The Inside Story of the Palestinian Uprising That Changed the Middle East*, tr. Ina Friedman, New York: Simon and Schuster, 1990, p. 248. This book is a useful complement to Peretz's book, but suffers at points from the Israeli perspective of the authors. They are at times overly concerned with the violent aspects of the intifada, of which there were undoubtedly a number, but far less than one usually sees with organized resistance.

17 Peretz, *Intifada*, p. 104.

18 For an excellent account of the invisibility of Palestinians to Israelis, see Yoram Binur's *My Enemy, My Self*, New York: Doubleday, 1989, an Israeli *Black Like Me*. Binur is an Israeli who pretended to be a Palestinian in order to understand the Palestinian experience. His invisibility to Israelis when he worked as Palestinian day laborer in Israel is striking.

19 Pappe, *A History of Modern Palestine*, p. 245.

20 We should note that the decline of the democratic movement in Palestine did not suddenly happen after the return of the PLO. There had been a decline before that, largely due to the isolation Palestinians suffered after Arafat announced public support for Iraq during the first Gulf War of 1991. The vitality of the intifada's 1987–91 years were never matched in the aftermath of that announcement.

21 A major cause of this ebbing of resistance is the 2002 Israeli invasion. It is described, along with eyewitness accounts, in Hamzeh, Munah and May, Todd, *Operation Defensive Shield: Witnesses to Israeli War Crimes*, London: Pluto Press, 2003.

22 Email communication to the author from Be'tselem.

4

The Zapatistas: From Identity to Equality

In 1910, campesino leader Emiliano Zapata decided to take up arms against the corrupt Mexican regime of President Porfirio Diaz. Zapata had been campaigning in the south of Mexico for land reform and against Diaz's economic policies, which concentrated land in the hands of large landowners. He adopted the slogan "land and liberty" (*tierra y libertad*). Mexican campesinos needed land to work and freedom from state policies that disenfranchised them. These demands were codified in the Plan de Ayala, a document that called for free elections and return of land from the landowners to local municipalities and the campesinos who worked them.

Zapata was not alone. In the north, Pancho Villa organized a military force, and in 1911, the coalition of forces drove Diaz from office. The reforms Zapata and Villa sought did not come to pass. Instead, the presidency was assumed by opposition candidate Francisco Madero, who demanded that Zapata demobilize his forces. Zapata refused, at which point the two broke relations. Madero, in turn, was overthrown and murdered in 1913 by a *porfirista* general Victoriano Huerta, who was overthrown in his turn by Venustiano Carranza. Throughout these changes, Zapata remained allied with the campesinos of southern Mexico, campaigning and fighting for reform and against the corruptions of both landowners and the Mexican state. In 1919, however, he was lured into a trap by generals from Carranza's army and murdered.[1]

Seventy-five years later, on New Year's Day 1994, the Zapatista Army of National Liberation emerged from the southern Mexican state of Chiapas. The Zapatistas declared themselves the inheritors of Zapata's legacy, adopting his slogan *Tierra y libertad* as one of theirs, and appealing to his words in their own writings and public statements. One might be tempted to see in the Zapatista struggle a local conflict over land and identity. In Chiapas, those who own the land are largely of Spanish descent, while those who work it are indigenous. This view would be in keeping with the strain of contemporary thought known as *identity politics*. In this view, the indigenous people of Chiapas, like African Americans, homosexuals, women, have suffered a particular oppression and are struggling against it. Their struggle must be recognized in its integrity and supported at the local level at which it occurs. Such a view would be mistaken, as Zapatista Major Ana María made clear in a speech in 1995:

> Behind us are the we that are you. Behind our balaclavas is the face of all excluded women. Of all the forgotten indigenous people. Of all the persecuted homosexuals. Of all the despised youth. Of all the beaten migrants. Of all those imprisoned for their word and thought. Of all the humiliated workers. Of all those who have died from being forgotten. Of all the simple and ordinary men and women who do not count, who are not seen, who are not named, who have no tomorrow.[2]

What the Zapatistas exemplify is not another local struggle over identity, but precisely the refusal of identity politics. It is in the name of equality rather than identity that they struggle. Although, as we will see, they adopt local customs and refer to local events, the Zapatistas never lose sight of the connection between their struggle and those of others around the world. It is no accident that Ana María, like Rancière, appeals to those "who do not count." Those who do not count have their particular ways of not counting that stem from the particular contexts in which they are not counted. But beneath those contexts lies a deeper solidarity: that of seeking to be counted where one does not. It is a particular genius of the Zapatista struggle to be able to retain at once the recognition of the local character of the indigeneous Chiapan resistance and the bonds this resistance has with so many others around the world.

The progressive politics of the 1980s and 1990s in much of the West were dominated by identity politics. The scourge of this politics has more recently become clear. It has ghettoized political resistance, undermining the solidarity across struggles that those who exist on the wrong end of power must rely on. However, we must recognize two things: that the source of identity politics was not a desire for ghettoization and that the way out of it is not yet entirely clear. I turn to the first recognition here, and try to show that a study of the Zapatista struggle can provide a model for the second one.

The beginnings of identity politics can be seen as dating from the late 1960s with the rise of black power and the woman's movement in the United States and the events of May 1968 in France. Previous to this period, left political struggle was, for most of the twentieth century, led under the banner of some version of Marxism. One way or another, one could reduce the various oppressions of contemporary society to class relations under capitalism. Racism, for instance, could be accounted for as a way to divide workers against one another, or sexism as a way to keep the reproduction of the working class intact.

The events of the late 1960s in the West revealed that Marxist class analysis could not account for the particularity of different oppressions or the integrity of the resistances against those oppressions. Racism is not simply a matter of working-class politics. It has a history which precedes and, while intersecting with, is irreducible to class. The civil rights movement cannot simply be thought under the categories of class struggle, nor can the women's suffrage movement, the gay rights movements, or the struggles of various indigenous groups in their various countries. In fact, one might argue, and indeed it was argued, that the attempt to reduce these struggles to a single one is itself racist, anti-feminist, etc. In France, the events of May 1968 led to the demise of the Communist Party itself, since it could not recognize the irreducibility of all other struggles to its own; in fact, it proved itself willing to turn against its own striking workers and align itself with the rightist DeGaulle government in order to prevent the emergence of these irreducible struggles.

There are different ways one might account for the fracturing of these irreducible struggles into what came to be known as identity politics.[3] One way or another, the history of this emergence illustrates Michel Foucault's claim that practices can have effects that are not only unintended by those practices, but run counter to their goals. Several factors undoubtedly played a role. The recession of the 1970s that led to a backlash against liberatory politics, the internal power plays and bickering of the progressive movement, the concerted efforts by governments to disrupt progressive struggle, all likely played a role. Whatever the sources, the outcome is clear. By the 1980s, progressive politics was splintered among a variety of groups that centered on the integrity of each struggle at the cost of solidarity across groups. This splintering both led to and was in turn reinforced by a migration of these splintered politics into the academy, particularly in the US The rise of black studies, women's studies, and queer studies departments, while offering important insights into the character of different struggles, failed to address the necessity of seeking commonality. That necessity, at least, was recognized, however inadequately, by the Marxist-inspired movements that preceded them. Instead, the focus become the identity and character of each group. Put schematically, the questions "Who am I?" or "Who are we?" came to replace the question "What are we struggling for?" on the leftist agenda.

At that point, the left lost its role as a threat to the status quo. The culture wars of the 1990s were a luxury item for the right. If all the right has to struggle against is the introduction of feminist third world authors into the cannon of Western education, then it has largely won the larger battles around the character of the state and the economy in the age of globalization.

Identity politics has not been without opponents and alternatives, particularly in the 1990s. Perhaps the most vibrant expression of an alternative was the inaptly named *anti-globalization* movement. What is inapt about this name is that the movement itself was, and to a certain extent continues to be, global in scale. It has encompassed workers, labor organizers, environmentalists, feminists, leftist political currents, and others from around the world. During its heyday, starting from the Seattle demonstrations of 1999 and for several years after, it showed various manifestations of resistance characteristic of different national and regional cultures. A better name for the movement would probably have been the *anti-transnational-capitalism* movement, if that weren't such a mouthful.

The movement, however named, cuts directly against the grain of identity politics. Whereas the latter is concerned with the integrity of each particular struggle, the former seeks solidarity across struggles against a common enemy. It recognizes that it is the same capitalist order submitting third world workers to oppressive and alienating working conditions that heedlessly contributes to global warming, the same alliance between corporations and states threatening indigenous cultures that prevent workers from migrating to countries with better economic or political conditions. We might say that the anti-globalization movement, implicitly or explicitly, has operated out of the presupposition of equality rather than the integrity of different identities. The idea that animates the anti-globalization movement has been that beneath the different political and cultural contexts in which people conduct their lives, there is an equality that must be recognized, and that it has been the movement's purpose to enact. That equality does not have a particular identity outside itself. It is, in Rancière's terms, "the equality of any speaking being with any other speaking being." First world laborers are equal to indigenous women are equal to third world child workers; and all of these are equal to those who govern national states and direct corporate policy.

In that sense, the anti-globalization movement would not have been an inappropriate choice for studying in this chapter. It illustrates the evolution of politics from identity to equality. I have chosen instead to focus on the Zapatista movement. Like the anti-globalization movement, it also operates from the presupposition of equality. However, unlike the anti-globalization movement, it has had as one of its central tasks the navigation between indigenous identity and universal equality. It has had to tack between the local and the global in more concrete ways than the already globalized movement against transnational capitalism. This navigation has not always been successful, although it has never been lost sight of. In tracing the Zapatista movement then, particularly in the years from 1994 through 1996, we can see the difficulties and possibilities of moving from an identity politics to a politics of equality, especially where the latter is not simply a rejection of identity (which, in this case, would mirror the policy of the Mexican government as well as earlier Marxist movements of liberation in Latin America), but an incorporation of identity into a global politics of equality.

We should not make the mistake of romanticizing the Zapatista movement, either by glossing over its difficulties or by removing it from its historical context. We will see the former later in the chapter, but at the outset we must insist on the fact that there were movements of indigenous political resistance preceding the rise of the Zapatistas and from which they drew lessons and inspiration. Resistance in southern Mexico did not begin on January 1, 1994.

Neil Harvey, in his comprehensive overview of the prehistory of the Zapatistas *The Chiapas Rebellion*, points out that there were large campesino rebellions against the landowners of southern Mexico as far back as 1712 and 1867. In both of these earlier cases, the rebellions were founded on a combination of indigenous religious symbolism merged with Catholicism. "Significantly, resistance was made possible by the affirmation of religious–cultural identities that were clearly not reducible to the political ideologies of either conservatism or liberalism. It was this space for resistance that allowed Indians to contest ladino [i.e. Western landowner] rule and affirm distinctive ethnic consciousness."[4] Although both rebellions were crushed, the appeal to indigenous symbols would not be lost on the Zapatistas. Instead, it would be integrated into a framework that, not without tension, sought to give place to those symbols and the local identity from which they stemmed in a larger struggle against the global capitalist order.

Closer to the present, during the 1970s and into the early 1980s, a number of campesino organizations came together under a largely Maoist umbrella. Although by the 1980s there arose the question of whether the leaders of that movement had sold out to the federal government, during that time the seeds of a unified Chiapan resistance were sown. Of crucial importance was the 1974 Indigenous Congress, which brought together hundreds of representatives from various indigenous groups across Chiapas. Their meeting resulted in a number of demands ranging from teaching in indigenous language to minimum wage standards to better sanitation. However, of greater moment for the later Zapatista movement was the integration of these various groups into a common arena where they could issue demands and discuss their intersecting experiences. Although, ultimately, the Congress's demands went unaddressed, their legacy remained, particularly in the Lacondon forest area from which the Zapatistas would emerge in 1994.

One characteristic of twentieth-century revolutions in Latin America, a characteristic well in evidence in the Sandinista revolution in Nicaragua and the resistance in El Salvador as well as in the earlier Cuban revolution, is that their Marxist inspiration was indifferent to the specificities of local conditions. What I am thinking of here is not the question that has long dogged Marxism of whether there can be a communist revolution in a pre-capitalist society. That question has remained with the Marxist tradition since the Russian Revolution. Marx saw communism as necessarily emerging from the capitalist order; the Russian Revolution, however, emerged from something more like a feudal order, raising the question of whether it is possible to have communism without passing through capitalism. My point, although not entirely unrelated, is different. The Marxist inspiration that has animated so much resistance in Latin America often seems indifferent to the fact that it is taking place in specific cultural and political contexts, where people see and engage with the world in accordance with their particular histories. Rather than integrate Marxism into the historical context in which struggle occurs, more often the historical context has been asked to bend in order to accommodate the Marxist approach.

One can see this at work particularly in resistance struggles in Central America. The Sandinistas, for instance, were often indifferent to the conditions of the indigenous Nicaraguan population. This resulted in tension between them and the indigenous groups.[5] By contrast, the Zapatistas opted to accommodate local traditions and customs. As a result, they not only obtained indigenous support; they also modified their own views of decision-making. From the Marxist-inspired avant-gardism of other Latin American resistance organizations, they turned to the more communal and consensus oriented approach characteristic of Chiapas' indigenous population. As the most famous voice of the Zapatistas, Subcommandante Marcos, recalled, "We had a very fixed notion of reality, but when we ran up against it, our ideas were turned over . . . We are a product of a hybrid, of a confrontation, of a collision in which, luckily I believe, we lost."[6]

This ability to integrate rather than reject local conditions is in keeping with Rancière's own rejection of Althusserian Marxism. Recall that for Rancière, the division between those who know and speak on the one hand and those who act on the other is the central characteristic of his teacher's Marxist approach that he rejects. To engage in a democratic politics is not to dictate to the people where their interests lie or how their struggle is to occur. Rather, it is to engage in struggle alongside them, intellectually as well as politically. Although, as we will see, the Zapatista struggle has accomplished this with incomplete success, it has oriented itself toward struggling *alongside* rather than *in front of*. This is a necessary condition for acting from the presupposition of equality. It is encapsulated in the Zapatista slogan of "commanding obeying," or commanding by obeying.

We can begin to see, although it will emerge more clearly below, that what may look superficially like an identity politics of indigenous culture is actually something else. It is the operation of the presupposition of equality. Rather than taking on the indigenous struggle as a struggle of specifically indigenous people, instead the Zapatistas have taken on indigenous struggle because of the *equality* of indigenous people. It is this approach that has allowed them to remain at once rooted in local customs and capable of addressing issues that concern everyone on the planet, such as the effects of neoliberalism.

And it is precisely those effects that spurred the rebellion of 1994. In 1998, Carlos Salinas de Gortari was elected President of Mexico on a platform of privatization, trade liberalization, and wage and price controls. These neoliberal policies converged with a steep decline in coffee prices from 1989 to 1993. We should note that this decline not only affected the general population of Mexico in general and Chiapas in particular. It had a special impact on women. As anthropologist June Nash notes, "Women's participation in the cultivation of the principal commercial crop of coffee is greater than in subsistence crops because of the intensive labor demanded in harvesting the crop."[7] The involvement of women will prove important both for the Zapatista struggle and for the tensions that have emerged between the equality they envision and traditional practices of indigenous cultures in Chiapas.

If the decline in coffee prices provided the discontent necessary for rebellion, changes in Mexico's Agrarian Law provided the precipitant. Most of these changes allowed for increased privatization of cultivated land. But the most notorious modification was the deletion of campesinos' rights to petition for land redistribution in accordance with the Agrarian Law's Article 27.[8] The modification of article 27 is in keeping with neoliberal thinking. It protects private property, thus integrating it into the global capitalist economy. It also shields landowners from claims that could be considered socialist in character. However, Article 27 has historically been a centerpiece of Mexico's self-definition and of the stakes of indigenous people within Mexico. Political scientist Nicholas Higgins explains that,

> the Mexican Revolution became a combustible mixture of elite dissatisfaction, popular resentment, foreign interest, and political ideology. Its greatest achievement was probably the 1917 constitution, with the inclusion of the all-important article 27, a legislative measure that restricted the ownership of Mexican land to Mexican nationals and in so doing provided for the redistribution of property so central to the agrarian demands of the rural masses.[9]

The change in Article 27, then, resulted in the immediate disaffection of Mexican campesinos – who in Chiapas are largely indigenous – from the Mexican economy and state.

Soon after the modifications to Article 27, the Zapatistas, who had been operating clandestinely in the Lacondon Forest of Chiapas, began preparing for open conflict. Anthropologist Lynn Stephen notes that, "According to Subcommandante Marcos and to the oral histories of other EZLN [Zapatista Army of National Liberation] commandants, at the end of 1992, communities working with the social organization of the EZLN voted in assemblies to give the Zapatista military wing one year to prepare for war."[10] Although not every community in Chiapas backed the referendum, support was strong. Between the decline in coffee prices and the legal sanction given to landowner encroachment, many indigenous campesinos were ready for armed resistance. As we have seen, resistance was not new to this region, and did not originate with the arrival of the Zapatistas. Rather, it was the Zapatistas themselves who were formed in the wake of previous resistance and who continued a tradition already characteristic of the region. Their particular contribution has been to continue that tradition through a subtle navigation between the local and the universal, between indigenous context and larger political developments.

The timing of the rebellion was set for January 1, 1994, to coincide with the inauguration of NAFTA, the North American Free Trade Agreement, which Mexico had signed in 1993. NAFTA provides for integration of the US, Canadian, and Mexican economies through the elimination of a number of national trade barriers between them. It was not solely the issue of trade barriers, however, that provided the symbolic motivation for the date of the rebellion. The lifting of trade barriers did threaten the indigenous economy by allowing for foreign investment and control. What was of more moment, however, was NAFTA itself as a symbol of neoliberalism, that is, of the penetration of transnational capitalism into all areas of collective life. Rather than recognizing the cultural specificities and economic needs of Chiapas' indigenous populations, neoliberalism would submit them to the needs and development of global capital. The modification of Article 27, with its implication of increased privatization and consequent dislocation of indigenous workers and campesinos, was inseparable from the changes that NAFTA represented.

Over the next twelve days the Zapatistas fought the Mexican army to a near standstill. During the year after the initial uprising, 88 of Chiapas' 111 municipalities experienced some form of civil unrest.[11] We will not spend much time analyzing the military aspect of the Zapatista struggle. Suffice it to say that the strategy of the Mexican state has changed from one of military victory to low-intensity warfare, with periods of larger-scale attacks, like the government's February offensive in 1995. It is described by Higgins this way: "pro-Zapatista communities have had to confront the terror of paramilitaries, the classic governmental tactics of using aid to divide and conquer, and the more constant intimidation that has come with the continued military encroachment on their villages."[12] Low-intensity warfare is designed not for military surrender but for economic deterioration: starve the population into submission rather than defeat them on the battlefield.

At the outset of the rebellion, the Zapatistas issued the first of what have been to date six Declarations of the Lacondon Jungle. "Enough is enough" is the slogan of this declaration, citing five hundred years of indigenous struggle against oppression. As justification for the uprising, the declaration cites Article 39 of the Mexican constitution, which states that "National Sovereignty essentially and originally resides in the people . . . The people have, at all times, the inalienable right to alter or modify their form of government."[13] On this basis, the Zapatistas declared war against the Mexican state in the name of "freedom and democracy." The twin themes of freedom and democracy have characterized all of the Zapatista communications. Perhaps more important, however, is the unstated theme of equality. This equality in struggle appeared first in the Zapatistas' creation of a referendum among indigenous communities regarding the decision to turn to armed conflict. The referendum is a repudiation of the traditional avant-gardist view that the leadership must bring the people along with it, because the people are incapable of seeing their way to radical action. In fact, it was the collective decision of the people of Chiapas that led to the uprising.

More recently, the sixth Declaration, from June, 2005, has sounded the theme of equality even more forcefully. Recognizing that in a democratic society it is the population that must rule rather than the military (in Zapatista terms, that the military leaders must "command obeying"), the declaration states:

> But then we saw that the Autonomous Municipalities were not level. There were some that were more advanced and which had more support from civil society, and others were more neglected . . . And we also saw that the EZLN, with its political-military component, was involving itself in decisions which belonged to the democratic authorities, "civilians" as they say. And here the problem is that the political-military component of the EZLN is not democratic, because it is an army. And we saw that the military being above, and the democratic below, was not good, because what is democratic should not be decided militarily, it should be the reverse: the democratic-political governing above, and the military obeying below . . . And so, actions and decisions which had previously been made and taken by the EZLN were being passed, little by little, to the democratically elected authorities in the villages.[14]

One might object here that "passing on" authority is not in the spirit of Rancièrean democratic politics, since that comes from above rather than below. Power is being granted rather than taken.

This would not be wrong; however, it misses the recognition by the Zapatistas, rare in revolutionary politics, that power indeed must come from below. Since the Zapatistas were in a position of military superiority relative to the autonomous municipalities they were fostering in Chiapas, they needed to create the conditions under which that superiority could not be translated into a hierarchy of authority. If, strictly speaking, we must balk at saying that in passing on authority the Zapatistas were engaged in democratic politics, we might say more precisely that they sought to create the conditions under which a democratic politics could take place. They did not grant equality, since that can only be presupposed by those who act. However, they shared the presupposition of equality and acted accordingly.

Turning to the specific struggles of the Zapatistas, according to Harvey, "The Zapatista opening affected struggles in four main areas: the rights of Mexico's indigenous peoples, democratization in Mexico, land reform in Chiapas, and women's rights."[15] Our interest will be primarily in the first and the last of these: the claims of indigenous peoples and women's rights. These two are inseparable from the other two. In particular, land reform is central to indigenous rights, and will be discussed in that context. By accenting the first and last of these openings, however, we will see more clearly both the movement from identity to equality in Chiapas and the tensions characterizing that movement. To anticipate, the emphasis on indigenous rights is a campaign for equality that does not lose a certain sense of identity, while the focus on women's rights is a struggle for equality that often cuts against the grain of identity, since it challenges the traditional roles of women in indigenous Chiapan society. (Here, however, we must be careful. There are many different indigenous groups in Chiapas, often with different traditions. Moreover, as Higgins remarks, given the various influences of religion, economics, and politics, "rather than the static, ahistorical conception of anthropological culture that has proved so damaging to Mexican Indians in the past, culture in this context should be understood as a constantly moving, changing, and evolving psycho-symbolic realm.")[16]

The struggle for indigenous rights centers on the campaign for autonomy. Nash points out that, "The autonomy that the Zapatistas seek is not the cosmetic autonomy of local rights but a recognition of regional institutions to resolve agrarian conflicts peacefully and legally, to give men and women (who had always been excluded from the land reform of the 1910 revolution) access to land through the offices of an Agrarian Tribunal that would be funded adequately in order to purchase an expanded *ejido* [land for campesinos to work]."[17] The "cosmetic authority of local rights" would be the goal of many identity politics. It would consist in official recognition of local customs and traditions, and perhaps an official acknowledgement of historical oppression. These are demands that are often not difficult to meet, and which serve as a substitute for a more comprehensive politics of equality.

The effect of such a politics is to turn indigenous groups – or other groups that seek a similar recognition – into museum pieces. Here we might appeal to the example in the United States of jazz. Where once jazz was created from below, largely by and always under the influence of African Americans, it has now become the stuff of Lincoln Center concerts. One might argue that this change has had the effect of bringing mainstream recognition to a music that was once neglected for reasons of racism. This is no doubt true. It is also, no doubt, the problem. Rather than generating the energy and creativity that it had during the first three quarters of the previous century, jazz has become more rote, less threatening, and as a result less interesting. It is no longer the kind of music that presses against the borders of the musically acceptable. It is now a form of entertainment offered at venues with high cover charges where ties and jackets are expected.

Jazz, of course, is different from the struggle of indigenous campesinos. However, the threat associated with identity politics is similar. To request the "cosmetic authority of local rights" is to retain one's traditional practices at the cost of becoming a display piece for the larger surrounding culture. It is to abandon the cooperative project of creating meaningful lives – the politics of equality – for a surface recognition of one's cultural practices, divorced from the lives in which they have played a role. What the Zapatistas seek, then, while inseparable from the identity of indigenous groups, is far from the demands associated with identity politics.

This autonomy is first and foremost a matter of land. The idea of land as lying at the root of autonomy did not begin with the Zapatistas. The expropriation of land from indigenous groups has been going on since the arrival of Europeans, and, as we have seen, has continued throughout the period of Mexican independence. If the change to Article 27 was one of the most important precipitants of the Zapatista uprising, it is because it blocked the possibility of campesino re-appropriation of land. The significance of land to farming communities should not, of course, be unexpected. (Much the same significance accrues to what the Palestinians, in their struggle, call the "right of return": the right not only to have a state but to return to the particular land that they were driven from during the formation of the state of Israel.)

Land provides three elements crucial for autonomy. First, it provides indigenous agricultural groups the economic resources for self-sustenance. When one does not have to submit to another economically, it is possible to form a coherent community among others one considers one's own. Second, it provides a space in which to exercise autonomy. This is not a metaphorical space, but a literal one. It might be easy to neglect this point, since many readers of this book are part of virtual communities. However, for those whose traditions require spatial proximity – that is, for much of the planet's population – it is impossible to maintain collective autonomy without a common space on which to exercise it. Finally, related to these two, particular land is often invested with religious or symbolic significance by indigenous groups. It is not only an economic resource that sustains or a space that provides for autonomy; it is part of the autonomous practice itself. This last element would be the one most closely connected to identity politics. However, it is not merely a set of practices or a sense of separable identity demanding recognition. It is instead a way of life that centers the economic, social, and political elements of that life.

One might be concerned here that what is being created under the rubric of indigenous rights is actually a more virulent form of identity politics. It not only asks for recognition of particular practices or perspectives, but ghettoizes entire communities from one another and from any larger struggle for solidarity. This is where some of the most difficult negotiating must take place by those who want to retain a sense of local integrity while at the same time fostering a politics of equality. The Zapatistas have worked hard to resist the isolation or self-enclosure of the struggle for indigenous rights, often coming up against traditional practices themselves. In particular, as we will see below, they have promoted an approach toward women's rights that, in the name of equality, cuts against the grain of at least some indigenous practices. However, they have not abandoned the challenge this negotiation offers, both in their own practices and in their resistance to the policies of the Mexican government.

In their own practices, they have adopted a number of aspects of indigenous culture. We have already seen the appeal to collective decision-making. This is a particularly significant adoption, since it is a place of intersection between indigenous practices and the presupposition of equality. In addition, there have been other appro-priations, both methodological and symbolic. Those who have read the writings of Subcommandante Marcos are familiar with his form of story-telling, a form that derives from indigenous oral tradition.

In addition, as Mihalis Mentinis discusses, the Zapatistas have incorporated elements of traditional Mayan metaphysics and epis-temology. One metaphysical element that has been adopted in Zapatista quarters is that of the *nagual*. "*Naguals* are animal co-essences that share a common spirit with humans. This belief in the existence of animal co-essences is so deeply embedded in the indige-nous understanding of what it is to be human that personhood, one's own character, idiosyncrasy, 'powers', talents, weaknesses and so on, are said to depend on one's particular *nagual*."[18] In many of the writ-ings of local Zapatistas, Mentinis notes, these animal co-essences are invoked to help understand the character of their struggle. Related to this are particular forms of Mayan animism, the view that every living thing has a soul. Although we cannot discuss the particular forms these metaphysical views take,[19] we should note that the ani-mistic character of traditional Mayan metaphysics brings it closer to nature and the land. This is not a particularity of the traditional beliefs of these local cultures. In contrast to more technologically developed cultures, those who roots remain sunk in the land often develop vitalistic beliefs about that land, since it is so deeply woven into their lives. (Perhaps an analogue of this vitalism is to be found in the emotional connection some people in technologically advanced countries develop toward their cars or laptops or iPods.)

Another, more politically forceful, appropriation of Mayan mythology has been the use made, particularly by Subcommandante Marcos, of Votán Zapata, an intersection of mythical Tzeltal figures with that of Emiliano Zapata. In Marcos' telling, which relies on his constant interlocutor Don Antonio, "They say that he [Zapata] is Ik'al and Votán, that they came here to end their long journey and, in order not to scare good people, they become one. Because they spent a long time walking together, Ik'al and Votán learned that they were the same, and that they become one in the day and night, and when they got here they made themselves one and called themselves Zapata."[20] The political edge of this intersection lies in the mytholo-gization of Zapata himself, which implies the mythologization of his political views. This melding of local metaphysics and local politics both offers a symbolic justification for the Zapatista struggle and an indigenous framework for conceiving the place of that struggle.

The other side of the appropriation of indigenous struggle is, as we have seen, in the demand for autonomy. This led to what was the most striking recognition of indigenous rights by the Mexican government, the 1996 San Andrés Accords. The government, although ratifying the Accords, never abided by them. Nevertheless, the fact of ratification alone testifies to the strength and orientation of the early Zapatista resistance movement. The San Andrés negotiations focused on local autonomy. The goal of the Zapatistas was to create institutions for local decision-making, particularly regarding issues of land, as well as indigenous representation on state and federal organizations. Among the principles undergirding this organizational pattern was that of pluralism. The following passage is from the Accords:

> Pluralism. Mutual treatment among the peoples and cultures that form Mexican society is to be based on respect for their differences, on the premise of their fundamental equality. As a consequence, it is to be the policy of the government to conduct itself accordingly and to promote in society a pluralist orientation, which actively combats every form of discrimination and corrects economic and social inequalities. Also it will be necessary to take measures toward the formation of a juridical order nourished by plurality, which reflects intercultural dialogue, with norms common for all Mexicans and respect for the internal normative systems of indigenous peoples . . . The development of the nation must be based on plurality, understood as peacefully, productively, respectfully and equitably living together in diversity.[21]

In this passage from the Accords, one might be tempted to see identity politics at work, particularly in the phrase "respect for differences." However, this would be a mistake. Immediately following that phrase is one that could be drawn straight from Rancière's writings: "on the premise of their fundamental equality." What bedeviled identity politics was not the respect for local customs and practices. Any politics sensitive to particular contexts must recognize those. It was, rather, the insularity of various struggles from one another. The problem with identity politics was that there was nothing to draw the various struggles into a common front. If these struggles can see themselves in one another, then they can intersect in a mutually reinforcing common front. The commonality can be predicated on a number of things. It might, for instance, be a commonality against a common enemy. This idea certainly does animate the Zapatista struggle. The name given to that common enemy is *neoliberalism*: capitalism in its unrestrained globalized character.

This passage, however, reveals another way to conceive commonality: through the premise or presupposition of equality. Rather than being united in what one opposes, the principle of unity underlies the various self-conceptions of local practices and customs. This, I believe, is how we should read this passage. The problem faced by the indigenous peoples of Mexico, and elsewhere, is not that their particular practices have not received official respect. It is, rather, the more fundamental problem that they are considered to be less than equal to those of Spanish descent. What the Zapatistas have sought to accomplish, and what the San Andrés Accords ratify, is that it is indeed equality that is at issue, equality in the Rancièrean sense of presupposing the equality of every speaking being with every other speaking being. This reading is reinforced by other passages in Zapatista literature. For instance, at the 1996 gathering of Zapatistas and international supporters in La Realidad, the Zapatistas issued a statement that was prefaced in part by the following words:

> The Zapatista Army of National Liberation speaks:
>   To all who struggle for human values of democracy, liberty, and justice.
>   To all who force themselves to resist the world crime known as "Neoliberalism" and aim for humanity and hope to be better, be synonymous of future.
>   To all individuals, groups, collectives, movements, social, civic, and political
>   organizations, neighborhood associations, cooperatives, all the lefts known and to be known; non-governmental organizations, groups in solidarity with struggles of the world people, bands, tribes, intellectuals, indigenous people, students, musicians, workers, artists, teachers, peasants, cultural groups, youth movements, alternative communication media, ecologists, tenants, lesbians, homosexuals, feminists, pacifists.
>   To all who, with no matter to colors, race or borders, make of hope a weapon and a shield.[22]

This premise of equality has the dual advantage in the case of the indigenous people of Chiapas of not only according a democratic character to the struggle, but also of arising from indigenous presuppositions themselves. As already noted, collective decision-making is one of the characteristics of the indigenous groups of southern Mexico. That form of decision-making reflects the idea that (except for women) participants in decision-making are equal, and thus that everyone has a say in the decisions of the community. Therefore, the presupposition of equality is, in this case, both characteristic of local customs and enshrined as an element of national struggle.

One might ask here how well the Zapatista movement preserved, within its own ranks and within the indigenous communities, the presupposition of equality codified (although later betrayed by the Mexican government) in the San Andrés Accords. The situation on the ground is, as one would expect, a complicated one. We have seen that the Sixth Declaration from the Lacondon Forest recognized that there was a tendency toward domination by the military forces, and sought to redress that through empowering the Autonomous Municipalities. We have also seen through the words of Subcommandante Marcos that the Zapatista movement has turned from the avant-gardism of previous Latin American Marxist movements toward a more egalitarian orientation. These responses recognize that there is always a temptation toward hierarchy in struggle, a temptation that is particularly acute when part of the resistance movement is armed.

In January, 1996, after the agreement to but a month before the signing of the San Andrés Accords, the Zapatistas made a further move toward egalitarianism by creating a new organization, a common front to stand alongside the military organization of the Zapatistas. The EZLN, the Zapatista Army of National Liberation, formed the FZLN, the Zapatista Front of National Liberation. The formation of the FLZN was officially announced in the Fourth Declaration of the Lacondon Forest. Among its guiding principles, the FLZN was to be "A political force which can organize the demands and proposals of those citizens and is willing to give direction through obedience. A political force which can organize a solution to the collective problems without the intervention of political parties and of the government. We do not need permission in order to be free. The role of the government is the prerogative of society and it is its right to exert that function."[23] Through its commitment to "commanding obeying" and through the fact that that obedience is toward indigenous communities who themselves are oriented toward egalitarianism, the Zapatistas have been able to sustain within their ranks and in their relation to the surrounding communities the animating spirit of the presupposition of equality. Although there have undoubtedly been inegalitarian elements, such as the division between military and civilian aspects of the movement and the media focus on figures like Subcommandante Marcos, there have been, alongside these, efforts to undercut the effects of these elements on the character of the struggle.

This leaves open the question, however, of the effects of Zapatismo on the indigenous communities of Chiapas themselves. Undoubtedly, the Zapatistas have received a good deal of indigenous support. As we noted, the unrest in the weeks following January 1, 1994 was widespread. However, it was not universal. Indigenous groups, like other groups, are not monolithic. There were supporters of the government among these groups, and the government, like all governments, has engaged in a divide-and-conquer strategy in local areas. In a study of the Mam indigenous group in southern Chiapas, Rosalva Aída Hernández Castillo concluded that, "The Zapatista movement has made it possible for some Mam peasants to strengthen their links to a broader indigenous movement through the new spaces created for discussion both in Chiapas and at the national level." On the other hand, she notes that, "Zapatismo has deepened the differences between those sectors of the indigenous community critical of the state and those linked to the PRI [the ruling party at the time] and the government."[24] This polarization has driven a wedge between the subgroups in the Mam community, and thus loosed its communal bonds.

Another anthropologist, Xóchitl Leyva Solano, sees much the same ambiguity. Studying the area of Las Cañadas in the Lacondon Forest, Leyva Solano writes, "Before 1994, the main social institution among the *colonos*, or indigenous settlers, in Las Cañadas was the *comon*. This institution was founded on a feeling of belonging to a community and was consolidated through various forms of solidarity and the achievement of consensual agreements."[25] Although it would be romantic to claim that there was a deep "communal harmony,"[26] there was some sort of consensus guiding the region. The Zapatista movement, by polarizing the community, has had the effect of weakening the *comon* in some areas in Las Cañadas. "In some communities it has been replaced by assemblies of ejidatarios with jurisdiction over primarily social and agrarian problems . . . Other communities have been able to maintain the *comon* because Zapatismo, as a new, homogenous ideology, has reinforced it and dissenters have left or been expelled."[27]

Zapatismo, then, has been, unsurprisingly, disruptive for local communities. This has been for a number of reasons. First, any movement for political change that gains purchase is disruptive of the status quo. Second, the Zapatistas have competed with local organizations by their mere existence. As we have seen, the Zapatista movement is not the first movement for indigenous rights. While weak, there remained movements and organizations on the ground that were in place when the Zapatistas emerged in 1994. Third, low-intensity warfare against the people of Chiapas has increased the stress on these areas. Fourth, one should assume that, along the way, Zapatistas have made mistakes at the local level. These mistakes have likely been less egregious than in the case of other movements. As local activist Gustavo Esteva points out, the Zapatistas "are attempting to create political spaces where all groups and communities can freely discuss their social proposals and establish their own forms of autonomy . . . In this manner, they responded to the double challenge of consolidating themselves in their own spaces and projecting that political style onto the whole of society without imposing it on anyone."[28]

There is another reason for the disruption as well, one that tilts Zapatismo definitively toward equality and away from identity politics. It is the focus on women's rights. Many indigenous communities in Chiapas, like indigenous communities elsewhere, have kept women in second-class status. (One might also ask how far the more technologically advanced societies have come in this regard, although it is undeniable that they have come some distance.) In its focus on indigenous rights and its deferral toward indigenous symbols and forms of life, the Zapatistas have steadfastly refused to accord women a secondary role. If indigenous communities are to be afforded the recognition of their equality, so must the members of those communities, regardless of gender. Although, as we have seen, Zapatista declarations are inclusive of everyone who has experienced marginalization, including homosexuals, on the ground it is the presupposition of and sensitivity to women's equality that has had the most profound effect. In this area, the struggle has refused to demur in the face of local tradition, but has instead insisted on a universal presupposition of equality.

Before turning to the specific ways this presupposition has played out in the Zapatista movement, we should emphasize the contrast between the politics of equality and its counterparts in identity politics. There has been, for instance, an ambivalence that many on the left have displayed regarding the wearing of the veil among Muslim women. This ambivalence is understandable, given that some women have publicly expressed a desire for the veil, since it shields them from appearing like sexual objects to men. The question of a principled stance toward the veil, however, remains open. In identity politics, the principle is one of respect for Muslim culture. The problem with this position is obvious. Much of traditional Muslim culture – and contemporary Muslim culture, for that matter – is misogynist. To respect a culture in its misogynist aspects is to refuse to recognize the equality of all of its members. Zapatismo has avoided this problem by emphasizing equality over identity at the core of its political commitments.

One might ask how easily the commitment to indigenous rights sits with the embrace of the equality of women. The problem might be put this way: in the case of women, doesn't the commitment to the equal rights of a group conflict with the commitment to the equal rights of particular members of that group? In which case, isn't it uncertain who should prevail? Isn't there a necessary violation of equality, no matter which side is chosen?

By implicitly embracing a Rancièrean view of politics, this problem is solved by grasping one horn of the dilemma. The equality of every speaking being with every other speaking being is an equality that must be applied within as well as across groups. A group that violates that principle is, on this view, violating democracy and is liable to political intervention. Otherwise put, identity must give way before equality. If one is to avoid the conundrums created by identity politics, this is a necessary move. To keep with the example of traditional Muslim culture, one might be tempted to say – and one would not be wrong here – that Muslim culture has been denigrated by the dominant Western powers, often, although not explicitly, in the interests of Christianity. Following from this, one might want to protect the integrity of that culture, seeking some sort of global San Andrés Accords for Muslim rights. However, if one does so without reservation, one runs headlong into the problem of endorsing the violation of women's equality. (This does not mean, of course, that women cannot choose to abide by various tenets of Muslim culture. The difficulty is that, as is well known, it is often coercion rather than choice that is determinative here.) One might cast this conflict as a clash of two identities. However, such a casting solves nothing. The Rancièrean solution is to privilege equality over identity both within and across groups, thus opening the way for a dissensus from the police order characteristic of traditional Muslim culture.

One might worry here that this solution to the problem returns us to the individualism of liberal culture. The equality of everyone and anyone, in this light, seems to be nothing more than the individualistic orientation of so many contemporary societies. Further, doesn't this lead eventually to the neoliberalism the Zapatistas have done so much to struggle against? To see things this way would be to fail to grasp the larger picture in which the politics of equality is articulated. The equality of every speaking being is not an equality that allows everyone to do whatever he or she wants. Equality is not the same thing as liberty. If it were, then Rancière's position would indeed lead one back into liberal individualism. But the politics of equality does not work that way.

In every society, there are particular practices and particular arrangements of power within and across those practices. Some of those arrangements of power are hierarchical. They presuppose the inequality of some relative to others. When one struggles against those inequalities, one does so as a member of a group (or of several groups). One struggles against the presupposition of inequality as it is imposed on women, or gays, or immigrants, etc., because one is a member of one or more of these groups. A *we* is formed out of a collection of individuals through political struggle. This *we* has, if we can put it this way, two axes. The first axis is a collective one: one is a member of a group that has been presupposed to be unequal. The second axis is at once collective and individual: one is equal to everyone else, who is in turn equal to oneself. Seen this way, a Rancièrean view of politics does not lead one to individualism. Rather, it leads one to solidarity, which is in some important ways the opposite of individualism. The equality of each individual *with* every other individual is an equality in collective action, rather than an individualism founded on the isolation and liberty of each individual *from* every other one.

In embracing women's rights, the Zapatistas have acted in accordance with this political framework. They have done so not only discursively, but also in act. This movement within the larger Zapatista movement has been called "the revolution within the revolution."[29] June Nash notes that 40 percent of the EZLN soldiers were women.[30] Some of these women have become spokespeople for the Zapatistas. As Lynn Stephen points out, this movement toward gender equality has been more easily accomplished among the Zapatista activists themselves than among the communities in which they operate. "While significant experimentation in gender roles may be taking place among groups of men and women who live completely separated from their communities while training as full-time insurgents in special camps, women in Zapatista base communities often continue to struggle for recognition and participation in decision-making."[31]

Perhaps the most important document detailing the Zapatista recognition of women's equality is the Women's Revolutionary Law. It was issued at the same time at the first Declaration from the Lacondon Forest, that is, at the time the Zapatistas began their armed insurrection. This means that it was developed previous to January 1994. For the Zapatistas, then, women's rights have been at the core of their program since before they burst upon the national and international scene. Alongside the lessons learned from indigenous groups, particularly that of communal decision-making, has been – in contrast to much of indigenous tradition – the presupposition of women's equality.

The Women's Revolutionary Law establishes ten particular rights for women: the right to take part in the revolutionary struggle to the extent of each woman's particular capabilities, the right to work and a fair wage, the right to decide the number of children they bear, the right to hold office, the right – alongside their children – to "primary consideration" regarding health and food, the right to education, the right to choose whom to marry, the right not to be physically abused, the right to leadership positions in the resistance, and all other rights and duties that pertain to other revolutionary laws.[32] Of particular interest here are some of the more domestically oriented rights, especially the right to choose the number of one's children and the right against physical abuse. These rights cut directly against the grain of much of indigenous practice. Indigenous women have often complained, particularly since the rise of the Zapatistas, of abuse and domination by men.[33] To enact at the outset of the resistance a document that goes against this aspect of indigenous practice demonstrates that the Zapatistas, while conversant with and oriented toward indigenous rights, were not uncritical with regard to the cultures they sought to protect. In the clash between identity politics and the politics of equality, they opted for the latter.

This was not simply a paper choice. July 1994 saw a Women's Convention in Chiapas that openly discussed and demanded changes to certain indigenous practices, particularly domestic ones. In addition to repeating the Women's Revolutionary Law commitments to choosing partners and protections from physical abuse, the Convention demanded punishment for rapists, recognition of property, and the teaching of husbands to participate in domestic work.[34] The frankness of these demands placed on the table a set of practices that had been ignored, partly because the entire indigenous population of southern Mexico had been ignored.

It would be a mistake to claim that the Zapatistas have been entirely successful in pressing their program for women's rights. Unlike the San Andrés Accords, there has been no equivalent agreement regarding the treatment of women. This is in part because the Accords were an agreement with the Mexican government regarding *its* treatment of the indigenous population. (Although, it should be recalled, the government began to violate the Accords almost before the ink was dry.) Women's rights are not simply, and not even primarily, a question of how the state treats women. It is a matter of how women are treated on the ground. This requires changes not only in the population at large but also within the populations alongside and in the name of whom the Zapatistas have struggled. As a result, women's rights have been subject to a negotiation that has not always been successful. For example, Neil Harvey writes, "Although a number of cases of rape by soldiers and police [during federal incursions into Chiapas] were denounced by human rights groups in the national and international media, the majority of abuses were covered by a blanket of silence. By 1996, many grassroots activists were perplexed by the weakness of the Zapatistas' own response to this issue."[35]

The situation of women, then, not unlike that of the indigenous groups of Chiapas themselves, is a complex one. It would be a mistake, a naïveté or a romanticism, to claim that the Zapatista struggle has rearranged the landscape of either the treatment of indigenous peoples or the place of women in indigenous societies, even in the most active period of 1994–6 that has been the focus here. Of course, such wholesale changes are rare in politics, particularly when the groups at stake are the most marginalized or disadvantaged. There has been a combination of hope, success, compromise, and failure in the Zapatista struggle. This is to be expected. It is a cause not for despair, but for nuanced critical appraisal. One must understand the forces against which resistance is arrayed, the strengths and weaknesses of one's own resources, and both the correct and incorrect moves one has made. This is particularly true from the angle we have focused on here: the tension between identity and equality. Since here the struggle is not only against what exists outside, but also within one's own vision and practices, the results are likely to be more mixed. They have been. This is not to deride the struggle, but rather to recognize the difficulties it confronts.

For the remainder of this chapter, I would like to step back from the complex realities on the ground toward the animating hope of the Zapatista struggle. The argument here has been that this hope is rooted in what Rancière calls the equality of every speaking being with every other speaking being. Although the terms used by the Zapatistas are often those of democracy, freedom, autonomy, and justice, it is in the end the presupposition of equality that lies beneath these. It is that presupposition that explains Zapatista declarations and practice. And it is that presupposition that is the stroke by which the Zapatistas have resisted falling into the trap of identity politics.

In a recent article, John Holloway writes of the Zapatistas, "A revolution that listens, a revolution that takes as its starting point the dignity of those in revolt, is inevitably an undefined revolution, a revolution in which the distinction between rebellion and revolution loses meaning."[36] The article in which this appears is entitled "Dignity's Revolt." Holloway contrasts dignity with traditional concepts of revolution. In his hands, dignity takes on several meanings. First, it arises within and belongs to those who revolt. It remains with the people, not with the leaders. This means, second, that it cannot be charted in advance. "If the revolution is not only to achieve democracy as an end but is democratic in its struggle, then it is impossible to pre-define its path, or indeed to think of a defined point of arrival."[37]

The reason the second follows from the first is that if revolt or revolution lies with those who struggle, then it is in their activity of struggle that its character emerges. It cannot be given on tablets from above; it does not come from an avant-garde who knows. "The traditional Leninist concept of revolution is crucially definitional. At its centre is the idea that the struggles of the working class are inevitably limited in character, that they cannot rise above reformist demands, unless there is the intervention of a revolutionary party." Dignity's revolt, if indeed it is to retain its dignity, must have a certain spontaneity or unpredictability associated with it; or at least the goal of the revolt must emerge from within the struggle, not outside of it.

But the revolt of dignity is not merely non-definitional. It is, according to Holloway, anti-definitional. It resists definition. "Dignity is and is not: it is the struggle against its own negation. If dignity were simply the assertion of something that already is, then it would be an absolutely flabby concept, an empty complacency . . . Similarly, if dignity were simply the assertion of something that is not, then it would be an empty daydream or a religious wish."[38] Dignity, in the terms we have been using, is the assertion of equality against identity. It is not in the name of a particular characteristic that dignity revolts.

It is not for the sake of, or only for the sake of, those engaged in revolt, for their particular needs or to assert their particular identities. Dignity is a concept that, because of its anti-definitional character, is inclusive rather than exclusive. We have, following Rancière, given some definitional character to the concept of equality: it is the presupposition that everyone is capable of building a meaningful life in interaction with others. I don't believe, however, that this definition would offend Holloway. Its minimal content is neither a platitude, since it points to a characteristic everyone who is not deeply damaged possesses, nor is it restrictive among people. And it shares with the concept of dignity the resistance to identity politics.

"The Zapatista movement," Holloway writes,

> has never claimed to be just an indigenous movement . . . Looked at more closely . . . the apparent definition of "Army of National Liberation" begins to dissolve. In the context of the uprising, the term 'national liberation' has more a sense of moving outwards than of moving inwards . . . It is consistent with this interpretation of "national liberation" that one of the principal slogans of the Zapatistas recently has been the theme chosen for the Intercontinental Gathering, "for humanity and against neoliberalism."[39]

To revolt for dignity – or better, to revolt from *within* dignity – is to presuppose the dignity of all those who seek to revolt, or who deserve to revolt. It is to recognize the oppression of others who do not share the particular characteristics that divide one from one's own oppressors. It is to recognize as brothers and sisters, as the Declaration For Humanity and Against Neoliberalism put it, "all the lefts known and to be known."

But if there is dignity, there is also revolt. There is, both in Mexico specifically and in neoliberalism generally, that which must be rebelled against. Dignity "is the lived rejection of positivism, of those forms of thought which start from the assumption that 'that's the way things are'."[40] The struggle on behalf of dignity is a struggle against its denial. And that which denies dignity does so on the pretense that there can be nothing other than what currently appears, that the police arrangements governing one's life are not contingent, but natural and inescapable. As Rancière has said, "The consensus that governs us certifies what everyone can see, coordinating two propositions on the state of the world: one says that we are finally at peace, the other announces the condition of this peace: the recognition that there is only what there is."[41] If we are to act out of dignity in today's world, in the world of what the Zapatistas (and others) refer to as neoliberalism, then we will find ourselves necessarily in struggle, necessarily committed to the idea that there is more than what there is. And we will recognize that there are those who benefit from the denial of dignity, from the suppression of that which is without definition, from the consensus that there is only what there is.

Indeed, it is precisely because it is without definition that dignity is so threatening. To be without definition in the way of Holloway's dignity invites a universality to the revolt of dignity. Anyone, any speaking being, can revolt in the name of his or her dignity, and can stand alongside others who revolt in that name. The demands of identity politics can be met more easily, co-opted more readily. Recognize the group's characteristics, honor them, and the task is nearly done. With dignity, with equality, it is not the same. First, because the recognition only comes afterwards. It can only be a response to an empowerment it is too late to subvert. Dignity's revolt is the revolt of those who already recognize their own dignity. Second, because it is universal in scope, because beneath the qualities that are said to divide us lies the solidarity that brings us together. Nothing is immune from critique or from change when the social order is recognized as contingent and its various oppressions bound together as a denial of dignity, as the refusal to recognize an equality already presupposed by those who resist.

During the period Jacques Rancière was writing *Disagreement*, his major theoretical statement regarding the presupposition of equality, the Zapatistas were practicing that presupposition in southern Mexico. We have focused on the central period of that revolt from 1994–6. We have seen that that revolt had roots; it did not come from nowhere. It also has a present, although that present has been diminished by the ongoing devastation of the Mexican state's low-intensity warfare against the people of Chiapas. This should not be surprising. If what has been written here is right, then the Zapatista rebellion, far from being a momentary cry of despair or a playful postmodern rebellion, is instead the articulation of a politics that has the power to place in question the police order in which we live. It does so not solely for the sake of local demands, although those demands existed and continue to exist: land and autonomy for the indigenous people of Chiapas and the surrounding areas. More pointedly, the questioning of the police order, the order of transnational capitalism and the states that underwrite its abuses, lies at the heart of Zapatismo. That questioning stands as an invitation to all those who suffer the indignities of its operation, an invitation to see themselves in one another and to act on behalf of the equality it is that order's mission to deny. It is no wonder, then, that, unlike the demands of so many forms of identity politics, it has become urgent that the Zapatista rebellion be suppressed. Or at least that the power of its message become diminished, which is the goal of all low-intensity warfare: not just to eliminate opposition but to underline its costs for everyone else to see.

What must be kept alive is the hope of Zapatismo, its animating message. To allow that to wither would be a betrayal not only of those who have struggled in southern Chiapas and those who have supported them, but also of ourselves. The equality whose presupposition has formed the backbone of the Zapatista rebellion places at stake our own dignity as well as theirs. We cannot dismiss the Zapatistas' struggle without dismissing ourselves, without nourishing those who act on the basis of our presupposed inequality. It is not at all certain that the people of southern Chiapas will prevail. The forces arrayed against them are strong, and the motivation to extinguish their message is powerful. It is, however, up to us to carry their message forward, whether it is in solidarity with them, or with those in Burma, Palestine, or the inner cities of the United States who struggle on behalf of their own dignity. The hope is that the presupposition of equality will prevail; indeed hope itself is inseparable from that presupposition. There are two questions that remain for us. First, can we institutionalize the presupposition of equality? Is it possible to make it permanent, or are we forced to live with it as a periodic but passing condition? And, second, what might be the future of this presupposition, given the state of our world today? Those are the questions confronted by the next two chapters.

Notes

1 For a full account of Zapata's career, see Womack, John Jr., *Zapata and the Mexican Revolution*, New York: Knopf, 1969.

2 Quoted in Holloway, John, "Dignity's Revolt," in John Holloway and Eloína Peláez, *Zapatista! Reinventing Revolution in Mexico*, London: Pluto Press, 1998, p. 189.

3 For example, see Michaels, Walter Benn, *The Trouble with Diversity: How We Learned to Love Identity and Ignore Inequality*, New York: Metropolitan Books, 2006, esp. ch. 5.

4 Harvey, Neil, *The Chiapas Rebellion: The Struggle for Land and Democracy*, Durham, NC: Duke University Press, 1998, p. 47.
5 On this tension, and the conflicts resulting from it (particularly with the Miskitos), see, e.g., Wehr, Paul and Nepstad, Sharon Erickson, "Violence, Nonviolence, and Justice in Sandinista Nicaragua," www.colorado.edu/conflict/5025/nicaragua.htm and Dennis, Philip A., "The Miskito-Sandinista Conflict in Nicaragua in the 1980s," *Latin American Research Review*, vol. 28, no. 3 (1993), pp. 214–34.
6 Cited in Harvey, *The Chiapas Rebellion*, p. 167.
7 Nash, June C., *Mayan Visions: The Quest for Autonomy in an Age of Globalization*, New York: Routledge, 2001, p. 114.
8 See Harvey, *The Chiapas Rebellion*, p. 187.
9 Higgins, Nicholas P., *Understanding the Chiapas Rebellion: Modernist Visions and the Invisible Indian*, Austin: The University of Texas Press, 2004, p. 102.
10 Stephen, Lynn, *Zapata Lives! Histories and Cultural Politics in Southern Mexico*, Berkeley: University of California Press, 2002, p. 141.
11 Nash, *Mayan Visions*, p. 185.
12 Higgins, *Understanding the Chiapas Rebellion*, p. 155. Particularly devastating has been the intimidation by paramilitary organizations loosely or informally aligned with the Mexican government. Examples of these are the campaign of Paz y Justicia in northern Chiapas, documented in the film *A Place Called Chiapas*, by Nettie Smith (Zeitgeist Films, 1998), and the notorious Acteal massacre, in which forty-six people were slaughtered. The latter is discussed in Stephen, *Zapata Lives!*, esp. pp. 324–7.
13 www.ezln.org/documentos/1994/199312xx.en.htm.
14 http://portland.indymedia.org/en/2005/06/320509.shtml.
15 Harvey, *The Chiapas Rebellion*, p. 200.
16 Higgins, *Understanding the Chiapas Rebellion*, p. 186.
17 Nash, *Mayan Visions*, p. 147.
18 Mentinis, Mihalis, *Zapatistas: The Chiapas Revolt and what it means for Radical Politics*, London: Pluto Press, 2006, p. 153.
19 Mentinis discusses these themes in depth in *Zapatistas*, pp. 152–67.
20 Quoted in Stephen, *Zapata Lives!*, p. 161.
21 Cited in Womack, John Jr., *Rebellion in Chiapas: An Historical Reader*, New York: New Press, 1999, p. 311.
22 www.ezln.org/documentos/1996/19960130.en.htm.
23 www.ezln.org/documentos/1996/19960101.en.htm.
24 Hernández Castillo, Rosalva Aída, "Between Civil Disobedience and Silent Rejection: Differing Responses by Mam Peasants to the Zapatista Rebellion," in Jan Rus, Rosalva Aída, Hernández Castillo and Shannon L. Mattiace (eds), *Mayan Lives, Mayan Utopias: The Indigenous*

Peoples of Chiapas and the Zapatista Rebellion*, Lanham: Rowman and Littlefield, 2003, p. 82.

25 Leyva Solano, Xóchitl, "Regional, Communal, and Organizational Transformations in Las Cañadas," in Rus et al. (eds.), *Mayan Lives, Mayan Utopias*, p. 165.

26 Leyva Solano, "Regional, Communal, and Organizational Transformations," p. 164.

27 Leyva Solano, "Regional, Communal, and Organizational Transformations," p. 167.

28 Esteva, Gustavo, "The Meaning and Scope of the Struggle for Autonomy," in Rus et al. (eds.), *Mayan Lives, Mayan Utopias*, p. 253.

29 See, for instance, Stephen, *Zapata Lives!*, p. 177.

30 Nash, *Mayan Visions*, p. 180.

31 Stephen, *Zapata Lives!*, p. 177.

32 Womack, *Rebellion in Chiapas*, p. 255.

33 See, for instance, the interview with Lieutenant Norma in Stephen, pp. 187–90.

34 Stephen, *Zapata Lives!*, p. 194.

35 Harvey, *The Chiapas Rebellion*, p. 226.

36 Holloway, "Dignity's Revolt," p. 165.

37 Holloway, "Dignity's Revolt," p. 165.

38 Holloway, "Dignity's Revolt," p. 169.

39 Holloway, "Dignity's Revolt," pp. 167–8.

40 Holloway, "Dignity's Revolt," p. 169.

41 Rancière, Jacques, *Chroniques des temps consensuels*, Paris: Seuil, 2005, p. 8 (my translation).

5

Institutions of Equality

Progressive movements have a mixed history of creating change. Sometimes they do, other times they don't. Often they create a lesser change than the one they had envisioned. Workers around the world fought for socialism; they got better hours and better pay. Women are in the labor force and in the public space (at least in some countries), but the limitations of what they are permitted remain evident. African Americans can vote, but economic equality eludes them.

It should not be surprising that progressive movements often fail, or that their gains are only partial. After all, progressive struggles are struggles by and for the oppressed. They are struggles situated among those who do not have power, among what Rancière calls the part that has no part. Progressive movements start from a disadvantage, from a position in the police order where the demand for equality would constitute a threat to those better placed in that order. That progressive movements, including the ones we have canvassed so far in this book, accomplish as much as they do is a testimony to those who engage in them.

One arena that has been most difficult to those involved in progressive struggle has been the creation of institutions that remain progressive. The twentieth century, of course, is littered with progressive movements that have created institutions that, once in power, begin to mirror those institutions they sought to replace. The history of Marxist communism over the course of the last century was a testimony to that. The anarchist Mikhail Bakunin predicted as much in 1873 when he wrote,

> Now it is clear why the *doctrinaire revolutionaries*, whose objective is to overthrow existing governments and regimes so as to create their dictatorship on their ruins, have never been and will never be enemies of the state. On the contrary, they have always been and will always be its most ardent defenders . . . they are the most impassioned friends of state power, for were it not retained, the revolution, having liberated the masses in earnest, would eliminate this

pseudo-revolutionary minority's hope of putting a new harness on them and conferring on them the blessings of their own governmental measures.[1]

Why is this? It is difficult to know for sure. There seem to be temptations of power that often affect those who gain some over others, although one is hesitant to make too broad a generalization here. It may also be that there is a trajectory of power – that the discipline of struggle and resistance takes on its own momentum and continues even where power has been seized. There is something as well, something to which we will return in a moment, that lay in the implications of Bakunin's words. Avant-garde struggles already start with a hierarchy, with a division between those who know and those who do not, between those who direct and those who are directed. That the distinction remains after state power has been seized may be less surprising when we find that it was there from the start. The state will not wither away when the struggle that seized it is itself hierarchical.

Of course, not all progressive movements have been communist in character. The problem many of them have faced is not that their institutions have turned upon those who created them, or upon those in whose name they were created. The problem has been that they have withered. It seems difficult to maintain a progressive institution. Think of the institutions of the 1960s: the Congress of Racial Equality, the Southern Non-violence Co-ordinating Committee, Students for a Democratic Society (although recently they are seeking to make a return). These institutions seem to have a short shelf life. Again, we might ask why this is. And here the answer is perhaps even more elusive than with the previous question. In some cases, of course, specific gains are made that render the existence of the institution less urgent. Another answer we might want to venture here, however, admittedly a speculative one, is this: the lack of an ongoing commitment to equality. This does not mean that it is easy to retain that ongoing commitment. Rather, the difficulty of sustaining such institutions may lay precisely in the difficulty of retaining that commitment. We will ask that question again near the end of the chapter. The suggestion here, however, is that there is something about progressive institutions and equality that needs to be investigated.

Progressive institutions, then, seem either to evolve into institutions that are antithetical to their original aims or alternatively to be incapable of sustaining themselves. Can there be such a thing as a progressive institution? Is it somehow in the nature of progressive movements that they cannot take on an institutional character while remaining progressive? In addressing this question, our aim will be narrower. What we're interested in is not progressive institutions generally, but institutions that retain the presupposition of equality. Our question will be one of whether it is possible to institutionalize the presupposition of equality. Can there be such a thing as a Rancièrean institution, an institution that presupposes the equality of every speaking being?

In many of his writings, Rancière himself seems skeptical of this. He writes,

> The community of equals can always be realized, but only on two conditions. First, it is not a goal to be reached but a supposition to be posited from the outset and endlessly reposited . . . The second condition, which is much like the first, may be expressed as follows: the community of equals can never achieve substantial form as a social institution. It is tied to the act of its own verification, which is forever in need of reiteration. No matter how many individuals become emancipated, society can never be emancipated.[2]

We should linger over this quote, since it contains an ambiguity worth investigating. The first condition of a community of equals is, of course, the presupposition of equality we have seen often in this book. The second condition, which he says "is much like the first," resists the possibility of institutionalizing this community. It must remain insubstantial. What does this mean?

On the one hand, if a community of equals can never become substantial, that seems to deny that there can be any kind of institutionalization of equality. Equality exists only in a collective movement, not in anything institutional that frames that movement or arises from it. For a community to be tied to its own act of verification, which is always in need of reiteration, seems to imply that a community of equals exists only in act, never in a static form. We might say here that a community of equals can only be a verb, never a noun. It is a happening rather than a site.

On the other hand, the following sentence says that "a society can never be emancipated." This might give a different reading to the passage we're considering. It looks here as though the concept of an institution and the concept of a society are merging into each other. If we read institution in terms of a society, then what can never be institutionalized is an entire society of equals. That is a much less controversial claim. To say that an entire society cannot be emancipated is little more than to deny utopian thought about emancipatory politics. It is to refuse the possibility that there will ever be an entire society of equals. Read this way, we can see why Rancière might say that the second condition is much like the first. If the first condition is that a community of equals is not a goal to be realized, then denying that there can be a whole society of equals amounts to much the same thing: there is no utopia to be sought, but simply a variety of struggles along a number of fronts, each one presupposing the equality of everyone.

Read this way, then, the citation leaves open the possibility of institutionalizing equality in a different sense of the term *institution*. In this different, more restricted sense, there can be institutions of equality, but never a society of equals. There can be institutions of equality within a police order, and there are better and worse police orders, but we can never get beyond the existence of some sort of police order. What must characterize these institutions is an ongoing commitment to equality, one that shows not only in the formal roles that are adopted by the institution, but in its unfolding activities. In that sense, any institutionalization of equality must display itself verbally, not just nominally.

More recently, in response to a question about what it means to say that democracy cannot be institutionalized, Rancière responded this way:

> What I mean is that it can never be identified with a system of constitutional forms . . . The power of the people is anarchic in principle, for it is the affirmation of the power of anyone, of those who have no title to it . . . Such power can never be institutionalized. It can, on the other hand, be practised, enacted by political collectives. But the latter precisely act beyond legal authority on the official public stage which is the power, exercised in the name of the people, of petty oligarchies.[3]

Here we can see that, in his current thinking, there can be more or less organized, more or less permanent, groups of people engaged in equality. What Rancière resists is something that would approach what he thinks of as a state, which he would likely identify with a police order. We might draw two immediate lessons from this. First, the state-form is necessarily hierarchical, and cannot therefore be a model for instituting equality. Second, and equally important, we may read the implication that, in conformity with the earlier passage, we cannot expect that an entire society can be arranged on the presupposition of equality. In other words, there can be no egalitarian utopia.

The claim that there cannot be an egalitarian utopia is a staple of much progressive thought. Among anarchist organizers that I have worked with, some would maintain the possibility of an egalitarian utopia as a possibility, while others deny it. However, the question of whether there can be an egalitarian utopia, a larger society operating on the presupposition of equality, can be asked in at least two ways. We must distinguish these two ways in order to avoid confusion in our thought about this. We might, using loose terminology, call the first way theoretical and the second way empirical. The theoretical denial of an egalitarian utopia argues that in principle there cannot be such a thing, while the empirical denial does not want to make such a denial in principle but rather holds that, given the realities of human history, the prospects for such a utopia seem dim.

We should clarify this distinction a bit, since it will have bearing not only on our reading of Rancière's thought about the institutionalization of equality, but also upon how we should think about the possibilities of progressive action. To say that it is theoretically impossible that there be an egalitarian utopia is to claim that there is something in the nature of politics that prevents it. Otherwise put, there is something about such a utopia that is in conflict with what it is to be engaged in politics, or at least in an egalitarian politics. This theoretical impossibility can occur in different ways. There may be a conceptual contradiction, something like saying that an egalitarian utopia is equivalent to a round square. Alternatively, there may be what is sometimes called a performative contradiction, a contradiction that arises when one tries to perform a certain action or say a certain thing. If, for instance, I order you to liberate yourself, and if you follow my order you've engaged in a performative contradiction. There could be something about seeking to institute equality across a society that would necessarily undermine that equality. That would be a performative contradiction.

The empirical denial of an egalitarian utopia is different. It does not claim that there is something contradictory or impossible about a society in which the presupposition of equality is operative. The empirical denial trades in the theoretical *impossibility* for the empirical *unlikeliness* of a society of equals. The argument is that human history gives us no reason to feel confident that a society of equals can be constructed. All attempts have failed, from socialism to communism to anarchism. What is the likelihood that other attempts would fare better?

This position does not dispute the very possibility of an egalitarian utopia. One might be able to give explanations for the failure of each previous utopian project: subversion by exterior forces, unrecognized deleterious power relationships, lack of adequate material resources. And one might argue that if the problems these explanations cite were overcome, there could still be an egalitarian society. To this, the empirical denial does not have a refutation. But this is not because the empirical denial lacks an adequate grasp on things. It is because the empirical denial is not in the business of refutation. For the theoretical denial, the question is whether or not there can be a society based on the presupposition of equality. The very possibility of such a society is at issue. For the empirical denial, it is not the possibility but the probability of such a society arising that is of concern. And, looking at human history, this probability seems remote.

Given the structure of Rancière's thought outlined in the first chapter of this book, we might ask whether his reticence regarding the institutionalization of equality is a theoretical matter or an empirical one. I would like to argue that it is a complex matter for his thought, but that, in the end, we should arrange his thought so that it winds up being an empirical matter. Seeing things this way will allow us to consider more clearly the question of whether there can be a society of equals, after considering two cases studies of small-scale institutionalization of the presupposition of equality.

On one reading, Rancière's thought seems to deny in principle that one can institutionalize the presupposition of equality. The reading would go like this. For Rancière, a democratic politics is always a dissensus from a particular police order. It arises within and in resistance to that police order. Social worlds are hierarchical. Every once in a while a politics of equality emerges within them. It may alter aspects of one social world or another for the better. But nevertheless, those social worlds remain hierarchical. They remain police orders. That is why a democratic politics is always a dissensus.

This reading amounts to a theoretical denial of the possibility of a society of equals. If a democratic politics must be a dissensus, then it must be parasitic upon the society from which it dissents. The politics of equality requires a police order as the context from which it arises. Under these conditions, there can be no society of equals, because a society of equals would not be a police order. Otherwise put, there could be no democratic politics in a society of equals. This reading would suggest a particular interpretation of the passage we cited above, when Rancière writes that a democratic politics "is tied to the act of its own verification, which is forever in need of reiteration." The interpretation here would be that a democratic politics exists only in act and without the possibility of being institutionalized. A democratic politics exists only as a struggle against the police order that denies equality. Once the police order accommodates the demands of that struggle, the democratic politics ends.

There is an important tension in this reading of Rancière's thought, one that threatens to undercut one of its most compelling characteristics. Before turning to that tension, however, it should be noted that this reading of his thought, which does seem to be in keeping with much of what he says about a democratic politics, threatens to cut against not only a society of equals, but against *any* form of institutionalizing equality. If a democratic politics must remain a dissensus, then it also must define itself against that which it opposes. The building of an institution, by contrast, has an internal dynamic divorced from its acts of resistance or struggle. There are a number of everyday tasks to constructing and maintaining an institution that have no reference to the reiterated act of verifying equality over and against a police order that denies it. Offices must be kept clean, bills paid on a regular basis, suppliers contacted, members kept up to date, etc. These tasks, which we will see can be done under the presupposition of equality – at least in small operations – do not refer to a dissensus. If a democratic politics must at every point be one of dissensus, then, it is difficult to see how any kind of institution of equality can occur, much less a society of equals.

And here we can see the tension with one of the central aspects of Rancière's political thought. What characterizes a democratic politics is precisely its rooting in the demos, in those who struggle. Rather than being granted any form of equality by a governing institution, the people presuppose their own equality. They act out of that presupposition. Politics does not happen to them, it emerges from them. Put another way, a democratic politics is one where the people take up their own equality, in contrast to the hierarchical character of the police order. Rather than relying on it, they break from it. A society with a democratic movement is, in many ways, two different societies in the same geographical space: one that operates by hierarchy and one that operates on the presupposition of equality. Rancière captures this idea, still utilizing the term *dissensus*, when he writes, "The essence of politics is the manifestation of dissensus, as the presence of two worlds in one."[4] Here, the dissensus appears not as a dissent from the police order but as the appearance of something else within the police order. The dissensus, which elsewhere in Rancière's thought appears as primarily a dissent, here appears as primarily the construction of a world, which is a dissensus only by contrast to the police order within which it makes its appearance.

If we read Rancière's view as resting on the idea of a democratic politics as collective action under the presupposition of equality, then its dissensual character becomes not so much a defining characteristic of such a politics as a secondary one. It is because societies, as an empirical matter, seem always to be arranged on hierarchical bases that a democratic politics is dissensual. That is to say, instead of seeing a democratic politics as necessarily dissensual at its core, we can see it as necessarily presupposing equality at its core, and in our world as always occurring as a dissensus from the police orders that surround us. Or yet again, a democratic politics, while not necessarily dissensual, happens always to be dissensual in a world that happens always to be arranged on various presuppositions of hierarchy.

This, I want to suggest, is a more productive reading of Rancière, because it retains what is most innovative and significant in his political thought: the idea that a democratic politics emerges from the demos. It removes any residual parasitical character of democratic politics from the police order from within which it arises. From the perspective of the police order, a democratic politics is always dissent. From its own perspective, it may be a dissent as well. But it is a dissent because it is based on the presupposition of equality. Dissent follows from the presupposition, given a hierarchical context. Dissent is not defining for it.

If we follow this path, then the reading of Rancière that it yields is a more empirical, less theoretical one. Put schematically, we can say that for Rancière, in our world a democratic politics is always (or almost always) a dissensus from a police order, since our world is characterized by police orders. It is possible that a democratic politics is not directly a dissensus but usually it is. The trajectory of such a politics is also unclear. It may be that there is a form of institutionalization that arises from it, although such institutionalization is difficult to maintain, since it requires the ongoing maintenance of the presupposition of equality. The ongoing maintenance of an institution of equals is difficult enough, and becomes even more so in societies characterized by hierarchy, i.e. all contemporary and almost all previous societies. The hierarchy surrounding societal interaction pressures institutions to become more like the police order within which they operate. Moreover, it is difficult to see how an entire society of any size could operate on the presupposition of equality, given the various hierarchies inherent in current police orders and the complexity of maintaining equality across a large number of spheres of social interaction.

This schema, it should be noted, trades in theoretical commitments for empirical ones. That democratic politics is dissensual, that institutionalization is possible but difficult, and that a society of equals is difficult to imagine: all these are empirical claims. By maintaining these as empirical claims, two things are accomplished. First, we preserve the idea that a democratic politics arises from the demos and is not parasitical upon the police order from which it, in some way, dissents. Dissensus is no longer a necessary and defining aspect of a democratic politics, but instead a secondary and empirical (if, under current conditions, pretty much universal) one. Second, it leaves the future of democratic movements open to the demos that creates them, rather than pronouncing on them from on high. It resists the temptation to say in principle where a democratic movement can or cannot head, but leaves it instead to the genius of the movement itself. This, it seems to me, is not only a necessary theoretical modesty; it is also in keeping with Rancière's own reluctance to have an intellectual pronounce in principle upon the tasks and roles of democratic movements.

If we approach matters this way, we are left with the question of whether, in fact, we can point to examples of institutions that operate on the presupposition of equality. And here we can answer in the positive. In what follows, I will present two small examples of institutions that seem to operate from the presupposition of equality. As with all the movements we have studied, that presupposition cannot be taken to indicate a pure equality. Instead, it is the presupposition of equality that seems to animate the operation of these institutions, one a food co-op and the other an anarchist book publisher. After studying these institutions, we will turn to a question that will likely be on the reader's mind: can these small institutions be replicated on a larger scale?

The first one is a food co-op near my home. In the small town of Six Mile, South Carolina (which, for those unfamiliar with Six Mile, is not far from Norris, South Carolina), there is a small building that, except for the welcome sign outside announcing it as the Upstate Food Co-op, would look like a lot of other rural buildings in the area. It is not a particularly large building, the size of a small house really. Entering the building, there is a cash register to one's right and a series of small aisles to the left. Squeezing through the aisles, one can find a variety of organic foods, health products, vitamins, spices, and pet foods. Walking from the inside to the outside, or vice versa, can be a bit disorienting at first. The inside, while crowded, seems larger than one would expect from the approach to the building. Nevertheless, within this modest house, a surfeit of food and health products finds its way onto densely packed shelves. Although I have not tried, I suspect that one can get whatever one requires for one's dietary needs at the co-op. There is produce, meat, and staples of various kinds. Moreover, co-op members can place special orders through the co-op.

The co-op was born not out of any desire for struggle or resistance, but rather from a purely practical need. In the mid-1970s, six families from the county of Pickens (which is where Six Mile and my home town of Clemson are located) decided to pool their money and order groceries in bulk so they could buy at lower prices.[5] In 1978, they decided to take their project a step further. They incorporated as the Share Food Co-operative, garnered other members, and started buying from larger suppliers in greater bulk. Originally, the arrangement was solely an economic one. There was no particular desire for organic or healthy foods. Over time, however, the orientation of the co-op moved toward healthier and organic foods, which have remained its focus.

In 1991, the co-op moved from its original location in Clemson to its current location in Six Mile. At that time, the co-op decided to hire paid staff. At first there were two workers, but soon one person became in charge of the store. This arrangement, however, did not work. From the accounts I received of this period of time, it seems that the introduction of a single paid staff member created a hierarchical situation that undercut the operation of the co-op. The staff member was said to have become territorial about the co-op, declining to share decision-making with other members of the co-op and operating outside the knowledge of the members.

After the experience with the paid staff member, it was decided that the co-op would run on a purely volunteer basis. There was a core of some seven or eight people, of whom one or two were more central, that helped get the co-op back on its feet, and from there an organizational flow chart was devised to ensure that tasks were taken care of. That flow chart has persisted up to the present, although it is currently being overhauled. We will discuss this overhaul below, since it is a lens through which the egalitarian operation of the co-op can be revealed.

Before turning to the reorganization of the co-op, however, we should linger a moment over its purpose and structure. The current structure was formally adopted in 2003 with the reincorporation of the co-operative as the Upstate Food Co-op. Its mission statement reads, "As a responsible member-owned and operated food cooperative of the local community, the nation and the world at large, Upstate Food Co-op is a crossroads of shared knowledge and a purveyor of its member households as a source of wholesome foods and closely related products at the lowest feasible price." Let's turn a moment to the member ownership of the co-op, because that's where its egalitarian character is revealed.

Membership in the co-op, which in early 2009 numbered around 350 households, costs a nominal fee of $24 per year. Every member of the co-op has an equal say in its operation, at least at the general policy level. Here is where the institutional character of the co-op is crucial. There is a board, managers and assistants, and general membership. All the positions are volunteer, with distinctions as to who fills what positions being determined largely by time and commitment. (I noticed that most of the people actively involved with the co-op were women. I have no particular account of why this might be. Some of them were retired women, and others of them working women. There are, of course, male counterparts to both of these groups.) One might expect that, with an institutional arrangement as traditional in form as this one, there would be a natural hierarchy that would fall out of it. In that case, the expectation might pick out as having more authority those at the top of the organizational flow chart, or (and this generally would pick out the same people) those who work more hours. This is not the case, however. To be sure, there are decisions made by people who are on the ground or who are more tied up with particular details (how many people are needed on a certain day or how to divide a particular foodstuff). But for the decisions that concern the character of the co-op, everyone has the opportunity to participate.

The reason for this is the presupposition that every member of the co-op, whether working at the co-op or not, is equal to every other member. Major decisions are taken only at general meetings, which occur quarterly. We will return in a moment to a particular major decision that has recently been made concerning the reorganization of the organization flow chart, but during a meeting I attended in December, 2008, it was put to the general meeting that the freezer was not working and needed to be replaced. There was a question about whether there should be a larger freezer with a transparent window or smaller ones that might be more energy-efficient. This question, which one might think would be resolved by the managers, was actually thought to be the prerogative of the membership, since it concerned the allocation of a good bit of money.

There were also other, more important discussions about the character of the co-op that were ongoing. One of them concerned the question of whether to continue to sell produce, which goes bad quickly if it is not purchased. Another, related issue concerned the effort to buy local produce. There were informal efforts to buy from local farmers (recall that Clemson is in rural South Carolina), but nothing systematic. During the time I studied the co-op, in fact, the produce manager left the co-op in order to concentrate on promoting and co-ordinating locally grown foods. Both of these issues were brought to the fore by the expansion of larger chain grocery stores into locally grown and organic products, particularly produce. Some people felt that this threatened the co-op with competition from the chains, which are more conveniently located for most people than the co-op. (A third issue of ongoing discussion was whether the location of the co-op should be changed to one more centrally situated, which would bring in more people but would cost more in rent.) Others felt that the fact that the larger food chains were moving in this direction was a victory for the approach to food advocated by co-op members. Of course, resolving that disagreement would not resolve whether the co-op should continue to carry produce or get more formally involved with local growers. But these issues offer some indication of the kind of decisions faced by the membership, and the egalitarian orientation toward the nature and operation of the co-op.

One might worry, however, that even allotting smaller decisions to people more actively involved in the co-op would undercut the presupposition of equality. This, I believe, would be mistaken. The presupposition of equality is not the same thing as the presupposition of identity. In almost every movement, there is some division of labor. We will see this again below when we discuss the anarchist press. The division is not inegalitarian in itself. It can certainly become inegalitarian, and one must be vigilant. For instance, if those who managed the co-op decided that vegetarianism was necessary for a healthy diet and decided to stop ordering meat, that would undercut the idea that all members of the co-op, vegetarian and meat-eaters alike, are equal. In fact, it would undercut the presupposition of everyone's equal intelligence, since it would instead presuppose that some are more suited to choose for others what their diets should be. However, that does not happen. In my (admittedly limited) experience with the operation of the co-op, there seems to be a good sense of the where to draw the line between decisions that concern the character of the co-op and decisions that do not.

One might press the issue here, however, and argue that even allotting the decision about that drawing of the line presupposes inequality. This, however, would fail to recognize how the co-op operates. Anyone from the membership can raise an issue at a general meeting or can attend the manager's meetings, which occur every couple of weeks. At the two membership meetings I attended, I noted that members were not shy about raising issues. Although about 75 percent of members do not volunteer at the co-op, non-volunteering members seem to feel free to raise concerns at the general meetings. This does not mean that everyone at the co-op is involved at the general meetings. The two I attended had roughly fifty and twenty-five people respectively (although the second meeting was held in inclement weather). However, equality does not come when everyone is forced to attend meetings or have input. It comes when there is an adequate space for input, which the institutional structure of the co-op allows.

One can see more clearly the operation of that structure if one follows the itinerary of a specific issue facing the co-op. During my time following the co-op's operation (roughly summer and fall, 2008), the co-op was in the process of a reorganization plan. The way the organization had worked was informal. There were day managers who assigned various tasks to the people who signed up to volunteer on particular days. What was done was what needed to be done, given the situation and the volunteers. Over the course of time, this led to a variety of problems. Day managers and others more involved in the co-op's day-to-day operations began to experience frustration a couple of years before the reorganization began. This was for several reasons. First and perhaps most important, the number of members volunteering was dropping, so those who did volunteer, and particularly people in managerial spots, started feeling resentment against the general membership.

Since, in the view of many, the co-op worked best when everyone co-operatively engaged in maintaining it, the question arose of how to involve more people in the operation of the co-op. Some people felt that members started shifting from thinking of the co-op as a place they were engaged with and started thinking of it more in terms of a place to buy things, as just another store. And if more people weren't brought in, the co-op would eventually either run out of steam or become the province of just a few of the more dedicated people, mir-roring the problem that it had had with the paid staff person.

There were other problems as well. For one, there was inconsist-ency in procedure. Since tasks were assigned on an ad hoc basis, there was no guarantee that things would be done in a uniform way. This led to confusion among those working in the co-op. Finally, there was some thought that the procedures themselves needed revis-ing and re-thinking, and a reorganization would allow for an entire organizational reconsideration.

From informal discussion, a committee was formed in June 2008 through the monthly managers' meeting to produce a proposal for reorganization. It consisted mostly of managers and others who had worked closely with the co-op. The emerging thought was that the organizational flow chart would be designed not by daily coverage, but instead by tasks. People who volunteered at the co-op would be responsible for particular tasks, and would become members of teams who goal was to accomplish those tasks. As before, they would sign up to work on particular days. But they would know what their tasks were before they arrived, and they would see those tasks as part of the larger operation of the co-op. This would solve two problems at once. First, it would make procedures uniform, since each team would develop its own set of procedures, and that team was responsible for that aspect of the co-op's operation. Second, it was thought that this type of organization would give each volunteer a stake on the co-op. The reasoning was this. When a person comes in to volunteer without a particular responsibility, they don't have a sense of their own contribution to the co-op. They are like extras on a movie set. They contribute, to be sure, but their contributions are not central to the health of the co-op. If people have particular responsibilities as members of teams, though, they can see why they're needed and how they help keep the co-op running. As the people I talked with emphasized to me, there was no guarantee that this form of organization would work, but it seemed worth trying. If it did not work, they would try something else.

In July 2008, an outline of the proposed reorganization was pre-sented to the general membership, which approved it, and empowered the reorganization committee to construct a final reorganization plan. From my outsider's perspective at that meeting, there seemed to be enthusiasm for the proposal. Although there were still details to be worked out, the membership empowered the reorganization committee to finalize the plan and present it at the end of the year, which they did. One of the details concerned the markup of the items sold. The co-op charges for items on a scale of markups, where the amount one pays is related to the number of hours one works at the store. For instance, on the old system, if one volunteered five hours a month, one paid 15 percent over the wholesale cost of the item, while if one worked two full days a month, one paid only 5 percent over wholesale. It was generally agreed that the scale of markups in place did not reward those who put in extra hours, and did not invite in enough people at fewer hours. So a new markup scale was devised that addressed both those problems. Although there was no separate vote on the new markup scale, the scale was presented at the December 2008 general membership meeting in case there were any objections to it, which there weren't.

One thing that struck me about those I talked with about the co-op was the diversity of motivations they had. One person said that they were interested in buying organic food cheaply. Another person told me that as they got older, they realized that they needed to eat more healthfully. A third person was motivated to get involved because they wanted to participate in a cooperative venture. This diversity of motivation might lead one to wonder about the extent to which the co-op is a dissensual operation. It certainly is, at least to my mind, an example of an egalitarian institution (or in Rancière's term, *collective*). Although there is a division of labor, and although some mundane decisions are taken on the ground by those working there, both the structure and operation of the co-op is subject to approval by every member, and every member participates to the extent to which he or she wishes. And, as both the old organizational chart and its reorganization show, it has a particular institutional structure. However, one might ask, in what sense can we call this institutional structure dissensual? And, in particular, from what hierarchy is it a dissent?

If we recall the original motivation for the co-op, which was simply to pool money in order to save on grocery items, we cannot reasonably see a dissensus at work. If the original co-op were a dissensus, then every time a few households got together to buy in bulk we would have a democratic movement. To my mind, there is a dissensual character to the co-op, but it is one that emerged over time and is a bit indirect. It is indirect in that its mission does not push directly against an inegalitarian arrangement, although its structure does. It is perhaps best to address the mission first, and then the structure.

The mission of the co-op is to make wholesome foods and knowledge of food available to the community at the lowest feasible price. As such, we can see the co-op as a part of the larger environmental movement. The relation of the environmental movement to a democratic politics of the Rancièrean kind is a complex one. One can approach environmental issues entirely outside of the framework of such a politics.[6] For instance, if a government adopts a policy limiting the production of greenhouse gases, this is strictly within the police order. It may be the case that this adoption is prompted by a democratic movement, but the adoption itself is not democratic. As Rancière stresses, there are better and worse police orders, and some police orders become better through the pressure applied to them by democratic movements. So it is possible to have an environmental movement that is not a democratic one.

It is also, of course, possible to have environmental movements that are democratic. The co-op is one example. Another one would be a movement of local farmers to pool their resources into, say, a farmer's market that would compete with the agribusiness produce sold in many chain grocery stores. Here there would be not only an egalitarian movement of farmers, but also a hierarchy that is being resisted. That hierarchy consists in the state's subsidizing of agribusiness, which the US government does in various ways. On this arrangement, smaller local farmers are treated as less than equal to farmers involved in agribusiness. A farmer's market, then, would directly be an act of dissensus.

What makes this example directly one of dissensus is that it involves the question of the equality of *people*. Rancièrean politics is a politics of the demos, of the people. This is what makes environmental politics complicated from within his perspective. In the agribusiness case, there is clearly a demos (local farmers) within a police order that sees them as less than equal to others (agribusiness farmers). However, many environmental issues are not structured the same way. There is, of course, the question of animal rights and our relation to non-human species. This is a crucially important issue, but not one that is dealt with through the lens of a democratic politics. But there are other movements as well, ones that *indirectly* involve dissensus. I believe the co-op is one of those movements.

Most members of the co-op likely do not see themselves as resisting any form of inequality. If they see themselves as resisting anything, it would be the hegemony of the chain food stores. The larger chains, at least at that time, were not providing the kinds of food that would meet the members'. This, of course, is both an environmental and a political issue. It is environmental because it concerns the structure of the food supply and all the environmental impacts that structure has, both on the ecosystem and on people's bodies. It is political because of the various political forces that sustain ecologically disastrous food policy and production. One would hesitate, however, to call it an issue of equality, at least directly.

However, let's turn the issue at a slight angle, and see it in terms of consumers and producers. In our food production system, the consumers are passive. They buy what is presented to them, choosing among what large chain stores, in combination with agribusiness, provide. In this sense, being a food consumer is much like being a voter. There are large, powerful, well-funded interests that decide what choices will be offered to people, who then cast ballots or dollars for one or another of those choices. In both cases, the whole thing is presented as though it were up to the voters or consumers. But, as many have pointed out, by the time the choices arrive before us they have been vetted by their respective elites.

Seen this way, the co-op is in fact a dissensus. It is a dissensus precisely from the system of food production that treats consumers as passive recipients of what large producers and suppliers are willing to put on offer. Although much of what appears in food stores (never mind fast food chains)[7] degrades the environment and is less healthy than it should be for the consumer, and although many people would probably object if they were aware of the practices supporting this mode of food distribution (an awareness that seems recently to be beginning to take hold), consumers are given no education and no say as to what they are buying or supporting, aside from the required nutritional labels. They are treated as though they were there simply to provide money to sustain the current food production system. Consumers are the demos of the food production system.

The co-op resists precisely this role of consumers. That is why the egalitarianism of the co-op is so crucial to its operation. If the managers and others more active in the co-op could decide for others on the best policies or mode of operation, then it would be simply replicating the larger chain grocery stores, just on a smaller scale. By creating a space in which people can participate in the ways and to the degree they would like, and where everyone regardless of their degree of participation has a say in the structure and policies of the co-op, the inegalitarian character of our current food distribution system is challenged. In this way, the co-op is an expression of dissent from that system. To be sure, this dissent is indirect. The more direct challenge is to the types of food on offer at the larger chains, not the passivity of the consumer (although there are likely some members who view the passivity of the consumer as a worthy motivation for participation in the co-op). However, in the dominant food distribution system the type of food on offer and the passivity of the consumer are intimately linked. It is precisely because the consumer is placed in a position of passivity that the production of food by agribusiness can be so egregiously harmful to the environment and indeed often to the consumers themselves.

It is perhaps here that we can see the process of subjectification at work in the co-op. Although, as we have seen, there were different motivations among those I spoke with regarding their initial participation in the co-op, once involved participants seem to see themselves as part of a collective venture. This collective venture is one that places them in an active relation to their food. There is a *we* that emerges, a *we* that defines itself through the activity of food choice and distribution. I caught glimpses of this *we* in contrast to a *they* – the larger grocery chains – during discussions of the latter's attempts to stock organic and locally grown foods. In any case, although the subjectification that emerges through the co-op is perhaps not as striking as it is in some movements of resistance, in particular those we studied in earlier chapters, it appears at the point at which the co-op's activities can be seen as a dissensus.

Although the co-op presents an example of an institution (or a collective) that sustains its egalitarian character, one might wonder whether that has something to do with the fact that nobody makes their living through their involvement with it. As we have seen, there had been an experiment with a paid staff member, but that didn't work out, partly because of the inegalitarianism it introduced. This can raise the question of whether it is possible to sustain an egalitarian institution where money is at stake. When it comes to maintaining equality in ongoing social structures, is it true, as they say, that money changes everything? The next institution we will investigate offers some reason to believe that it is possible for people to make a living through an egalitarian institution. Granted, the money isn't much. However, it seems possible, even within the context of an overriding capitalist environment of the kind that exists in the US, to keep in operation an institution in which paid work can be had without the creation of a hierarchical system.

AK Press is located in the urban core of Oakland, California. It is a few blocks from the Greyhound Station and across the street from the St. Vincent de Paul soup kitchen. Its 6,000 square foot warehouse is operated by eight employees, five of them full-time, and several volunteers. There is a ninth employee located in Baltimore who does publicity for the Press. Together they form a collective, in much the same way as the workers at the Upstate Food Co-op form a collective. (There is also a small sister group in Edinburgh, Scotland, currently with two employees.) Their statement of purpose reads: "AK Press exists to publish and distribute materials that contribute to social and political changes based on Anarchist principles. These principles integrate the abolition of government, the destruction of capitalism, and the replacement of hierarchies and prejudices by constructing egalitarian structures based on freedom, equality, and self-determination. We do not seek to merely criticize or escape the existing state of the world, but to offer and function as a better alternative."

The press has had up to a dozen employees, and would like to hire another worker or two, but with the recent downturn in the economy, funds are tight.[8] It publishes around twenty new titles a year, mostly but not exclusively on anarchist themes. Over the past several years, the press has sold an average of 70,000 copies of AK Press books. In addition to its own books, however, it also distributes books for other publishers, carrying roughly three to four thousand other titles. The distribution end of the press offers several services. It sells books through the AK Press catalogue, acts as the exclusive distributor for some smaller presses, and helps mainstream publishers of anarchist-oriented books by offering those books on their websites and through tabling at events.

What is most striking about the press is not only the anarchist orientation of its list, but the anarchist mode of operation of the press itself. Not only is everyone paid the same per-hour salary, all decisions of any note are taken by the collective. The formal structure of decision-making around publishing is this. If someone wants to publish with AK Press, he or she sends a proposal or a manuscript. That proposal or manuscript is reviewed by one of the members of the collective involved in publishing (somebody on the publishing side usually volunteers for this task), and then brought before the other members of the publishing side of AK Press, which includes the publicist from Baltimore who is present by speaker phone. If the members from the publishing side think that the work should go to the next step, it is then put before the entire collective. At this stage in the process, people are pretty generous about allowing proposals and manuscripts to go forward, since they might be of interest to one or another of the members of the entire collective. Essentially, their work consists in discarding works that are clearly inappropriate for the AK's list.

If the proposed work reaches the next stage, the person who reviewed it presents it to the collective as a whole, where it is discussed again. There is a vote as to whether the manuscript should be reviewed by one or two people in the collective. In the meeting I attended, several of the proposed works struck the interest of different members of the collective, who volunteered to review the manuscript. Before reviewing each one, however, a vote of the collective is taken to assess whether the collective as a whole thinks the manuscript merits this second, more thorough, review. With nine members of the collective, if the vote is close, say five to four, further discussion occurs. Otherwise, the decision of the collective either moves the work forward or stops it there.

There is then a third stage. When a manuscript is reviewed, it is once again summarized before the collective, where discussion and voting occur. There were no manuscripts at this stage at the meeting I attended, but I was told that these discussions are more involved, since it is at this point that manuscripts are accepted for publication. However, the process remains the same: voting, and in case of a close vote, more discussion. When manuscripts reach this point in the process, there are three criteria usually in play regarding whether manuscripts are accepted or not: political merit, financial considerations (whether there is enough money to put into the book, given what it might retrieve in sales), and the labor it would take to produce the book (e.g. how much editing the manuscript requires). One person said that, at least to their knowledge, financial considerations have never trumped political merit, although labor considerations have.

One might worry that by allowing voting rather than requiring consensus at the various stages of review, there might arise a problem of factions within the press. We will return to the question of voting versus consensus below, but I should note that this did not seem to be a problem for the collective. Although voting is the bottom line, there seems to be an attempt to reach consensus through compromise wherever possible. For instance, one of the works put before the entire collective for review at the meeting I attended was a proposal without a manuscript. There was both some interest and some hesitation about whether to take the proposal to the next stage. Several members of the collective wanted to wait until the next meeting, two weeks away, to review the proposal more closely. There was concern, however, that if the review was postponed, the author would go with another publisher, and that militated toward a positive vote on the manuscript at the meeting. After discussion, it was proposed that there be a quick meeting the following week to decide whether to review the work, and this was accepted by everyone in the collective. I was told that this method of proceeding was common within the press, and since many of the people in the collective had been members of other anarchist collectives before arriving at AK, they understood the importance of accommodating divergent viewpoints where possible.

Although anarchist in orientation and operation, in accordance with its statement of purpose, AK Press is not exclusively anarchist in what it publishes. One member of the collective told me that the press seemed to focus on three themes: contemporary progressive movements, anarchist history, and, to a lesser extent, cultural issues such as radical parenting or punk music. From my discussions with members of the press (I was able to talk with five members of the collective), it became clear, particularly among those involved in the publishing end, that the goal of the press was to contribute to the current political context (widely defined) from an anarchist perspective rather than simply to publish anarchist texts. Although unlikely to publish or distribute books that stray very far from anarchist principles – John Rawls will not likely appear on their list soon – members of the collective are not rigid or doctrinaire in their decisions about what to publish. Moreover, since each member of the collective is considered by the others to be equal, the specific interests of each have a bearing on what is published. There is an effort, then, to respond to issues such as race or gender in ways that intersect (even if they don't entirely converge) with an anarchist orientation. In the meeting I attended where manuscript proposals were discussed, it was clear that people chose to read works that interested them, which in turn influences what is ultimately published by the press.

Since AK Press is operated collectively, not only what it publishes but how it operates on a day-to-day level is decided by the members of the collective. Several members of the collective emphasized to me that everything the press does is reviewable. There have been discussions recently, although no decision taken, as to whether to change from decision-by-vote to decision-by-consensus. This open form of operation means that the press is, in a deeper way than most institutions, a product of those who are working within it, and changes with the composition of the collective. There is a fluidity to its structure, which should not, however, be confused with chaos. At least two elements keep the changes AK undergoes framed within particular boundaries. These two elements would seem likely to be found in any longstanding institution that seeks to function on the basis of equality. The first concerns the composition of its membership, and the second its institutional trajectory.

All of the members of AK that I interviewed had a background of some sort in anarchism. Some were members of anarchist collectives previous to associating themselves with the press, but all of them had some awareness of anarchist principles. (All of them also had an interest in books in general and an interest in AK's list in particular previous to working with the press.) In essence, then, those who worked with the press were already "groomed" to navigate collective decision-making. They understood through experience, whether positive or negative, what it means to work without an authority overseeing them and how to see fellow members as equal participants in a collective activity. This does not mean, of course, that everyone who has passed through the press was amenable to its particular orientation. But, given the ethos of the press as well as its voting structure, there is a self-selection that operates to garner certain kinds of people and to discourage people who do not fit well into the collective mold. Several of the people I interviewed also noted that before joining the collective, they did volunteer work with the press. This, of course, acts as another form of vetting.

The institutional trajectory of the press concerns the weight of its previous history. Although all policies and procedures (at least those that don't violate its founding principles) can be discussed, reviewed, and changed by members, everyone who works at the press does so on the basis of institutional arrangements that are already in place. This means that decisions are not made *ex nihilo*, but rather against the background of an operation that is already in motion. The significance of this should not be underestimated. Rather than deciding each day how to go about the work of the collective, AK Press's members come into an institutional arrangement that structures how they are to proceed. From there, any member of the collective can raise for discussion a particular policy or procedure. But that discussion happens within a context that allows it to be framed. The boat does not continually have to be rebuilt while it is at sea. It already exists, and the questions facing the collective about its operation concern the planks of which it is made, the strength of the mast, the direction in which it may be sailing. But the members are not individually afloat in the water wondering each day how to make a structure that will get them somewhere.

There is a particular issue that arose in the course of my interviews with collective members that illustrates the dynamic of institutional structure and change. Up until 2005–6, all members of the collective worked in both publishing and distribution. That is to say, they were involved both in the initial review of manuscripts and seeing them along to publication as well as in the decisions and labor concerning what other presses' books to distribute. This ensured participation by each member of the collective in all aspects of AK's operation. However, it was decided at that time to split the distribution and publishing ends of the press. This decision was taken for the sake of efficiency, since it was thought that having people develop expertise in a slightly narrower area would make each end of the press's operation run more smoothly. The distinction is not a hard and fast one; for instance, one member of the distribution end of the collective told me that she had recently designed the cover for a book, a task usually reserved for the publishing end. However, the division of labor was noticeable, even to me. The people involved in distribution tended to cluster more among the stacks of books at one end of the warehouse, while those involved in publishing were more nearly gathered at the other end, where most of the computers are.

The decision to divide the press's operation, however, is not one that everyone is entirely comfortable with. This is not to say that anyone is entirely opposed to it. In my discussions, nobody said it was a bad idea. However, it came up several times as a major change in AK's operation, and people seemed to think that there were considerations on both sides of the issue. On the one hand, there did seem to be greater efficiency associated with the division of labor, which not only accomplished more in less time but also allowed the extra time to be used to focus on the political character of the press. With more time, people could think and discuss with one another in a more leisurely way the character of the press and where it is and should be headed. On the other hand, there seemed to be a lingering worry about whether the division of labor would in some way split the collective into two groups with barriers of communication between them. There are, as mentioned, projects engaged in by the entire collective, in particular the centrally important one of deciding which books to publish under AK's imprint. However, divisions of labor can have a way of distancing people from one another, and this was a vague worry expressed by several people during our interviews.

This worry intersects with another one. When conflicts arise in the press over how to handle various issues, there is, behind these conflicts, the question of their source. What part of these conflicts is structural and what part interpersonal? In other words, if there is a conflict, how much of it requires a collective thinking about the character of the press and a review of its policies, and how much of it reflects the state of interpersonal relationships at the moment? To the degree that it is the latter, it should probably be approached interpersonally, as a conflict between two or more people that needs resolution between or among them. Alternatively, if there is a tension between the current members of the collective and the structure within which they are working, then the proper form of resolution would be to review the current policies and procedures in order to revise them in a fashion that better reflects the current character of the collective. One can see how this issue could be reflected in concerns about divisions of labor at the press. If a conflict were to arise regarding the division of labor, one of the questions to be asked would be how much this reflects a problem with the division itself and how much is a matter of the interpersonal relationships among those operating on different sides of the division. And, of course, there is no bright line to distinguish in a particular conflict which form of resolution would be best.

This is a particularly difficult issue to navigate in a mode of operation where decisions and policies are revisable. In a traditional institutional structure, the question of conflict is always reduced to interpersonal terms. Where there is a problem, the people involved in the problem must work it out. The structure of the organization is, unless a deep crisis develops, taken as given. It forms the frame within which conflicts must be worked out. (If I may be permitted this speculation, I suspect that this is not irrelevant to the fact that so many of these conflicts seem to take on the character of sibling fights. Having little control of one's institutional surroundings, one can only take out one's frustrations on one's peers or subordinates, with the institution taking on the role of the parental authority figure that steps in and resolves the conflict.) At operations like AK, however, the question of structural weakness versus interpersonal difficulty – or some combination of both – often cannot be answered with assurance. As a result, there is a constant negotiation between and among these possibilities when conflict arises.

So far in the history of AK, the questions such an egalitarian form of operation raises seem to have been confronted successfully. The press has been in formal operation since 1990, and has survived the loss of its founding members. This latter fact is significant in thinking about ongoing institutions of equality, since it shows that the institutional structure of AK is not simply a product of its initial membership but can support different personalities within it. Moreover, given that that structure allows for revising particular decisions, it seems to be at once flexible and accommodating and, at the same time, to provide of a framework that allows accommodations to be carried out within a stable and recognizable trajectory.

Before closing with some larger issues that the discussion of the Upstate Food Co-op and AK Press raise, it would be worth pausing a moment over the press as a mode of subjectification and a process of dissensus. The latter is a stated objective of the press and of its members. It is important to emphasize, however, that the dissensus occurs on two levels, both of which are Rancièrean, but in distinct senses. The first level involves the content of AK's publications. The press seeks to promote anarchist principles, which, as its founding principles state, "integrate the abolition of government, the destruction of capitalism, and the replacement of hierarchies and prejudices by constructing egalitarian structures based on freedom, equality, and self-determination." It is the mission of AK Press to agitate through publication for a society whose participants recognize one another as equals. This, of course, is a dissensus from the current social arrangement, and the members of the collective see it as such (although, unless they've read much Rancière, they probably don't use the term *dissensus* to describe their views). They oppose the inegalitarian arrangements characteristic of our society, from its racism and its sexism to its treatment of workers, immigrants, the poor, and others.

This is in contrast to the membership of the co-op. There were a couple of people from the co-op I spoke with who would likely have some sympathy for the principles of AK Press, although perhaps not entirely. Most, however, did not seem to see themselves as resistors to current social arrangements, except for some aspects of its food distribution. The larger critique of capitalism and hierarchy that AK's members promote would be foreign to many involved with the co-op. The lesson we should draw from this, however, is not that the latter is not dissensual while the former is. Rather, it is that dissensus occurs in the name of equality even where it might not be seen to do so. The Upstate Food Co-op, as I have argued, is in fact a dissensus, one that involves resistance to the pacification of consumers in the name of their active equality. What the collective at AK Press has done is to embed activities like those of the co-op into a larger critique of hierarchy, of the police order. In doing so, they have offered a particular framework for understanding activities like those of the co-op, a framework that the members of the co-op might or might not, given the chance to reflect on it, endorse. In any case, there is nothing in the operation of the co-op that would be foreign to the political views promoted by AK Press, even if AK's ideas would not be immediately embraced by those involved in that operation.

This brings us to the second Rancièrean level of AK Press: its own operation. AK does not only promote egalitarianism, it also enacts it. It explicitly structures its internal operations to reflect the kind of society it is trying to promote. The AK collective seeks egalitarianism, and believes that in order accomplish that goal it must embody it in its own operations. Therefore, it structures itself in accordance with the presupposition of the equality of every speaking being involved with it, that is to say with every member of the press. We have seen how that happens, and how the difficulties the collective reflects upon are difficulties associated with maintaining that presupposition in the face of changing membership and the evolving goals and interests of that membership. In contrast to progressive groups that are more avant-gardist, seeking to liberate society from capitalism through more hierarchical forms of operation, AK Press, in accordance with its anarchist principles, operates on the assumption that liberation starts at home. One cannot call for the liberation of others from our society's police order by means of the construction of an alternative hierarchy with a promise of equality to come later. Egalitarianism, if it is to be had, must be integrated into the process of dissensus rather than lying at the end as a goal.

Because the members of AK's collective see themselves this way, and because most (if not all) of them had an anarchist orientation before their involvement with the press, the mode of subjectification of the collective is less starkly in evidence than it would be for many other movements. Compared, for instance, with the US civil rights movement, the collective sense of exhilaration in seeing oneself as a group in action on the presupposition of its equality is less striking. However, although less striking, it is there nevertheless. I asked several members of the press about whether they saw AK as realizing the hopes they might have had for an anarchist organization. They were all in agreement that AK provides a model for such organization. They all insisted that maintaining the press as such an organization was not an easy task. It involves navigating the conflicts and difficulties mentioned above. That, however, seems to be less an obstacle to than a requirement of egalitarian institutions.

This maintenance itself illustrates an aspect of Rancière's conception of subjectification. As we have seen, subjectification is, in his view, more of a process than a substance. Subjectification is the name of what people do rather than (or more than) who they become. It is a collective expression of the presupposition of equality, and as such is tied to the activities through which it is expressed. The fluid character of AK's operations is an example of this. For the collective, maintaining the presupposition of equality requires an openness to the evolution of the membership and of that membership's interests and involvements. There is no point at which one arrives that can stand as the terminal place for the building of an egalitarian structure. Or, to put the matter another way, the maintenance of an egalitarian institution is itself a process of subjectification rather than simply a product of an egalitarian institutional framework. As Rancière puts the point in questioning the possibility of institutionalizing democratic movements, the press "is tied to the act of its own verification, which is forever in need of reiteration." This does not mean, of course, that the framework is irrelevant. AK Press does have, after all, founding principles and a small set of operating principles.[9] However, those principles are designed to foster the process of subjectification rather than to impede the process in the name of an equality that, in the end, can only be had through the attention and flexibility that the presupposition of equality requires.

The Upstate Food Co-op and AK Press seem to show that it is possible to institutionalize or collectivize the presupposition of equality. While the co-op was not structured on the basis of a dissensus from an inegalitarian situation, it is, as we saw, a challenge to the police order inherent in the dominant food production and distribution system. AK Press, however, does see itself involved in a dissensus, both from the structure and from the orientation of book publishing as well as capitalism in general. We could end the discussion here, claiming that since there can be egalitarian institutions, even in the midst of the police orders that govern us, we have answered the driving question of this chapter. However, there is and should be a remaining doubt about what has been discussed here. Both of the institutions we have canvassed share a particular quality: they are very small institutions. Upstate Food Co-op only has a handful of people working at any given time, and its managers (those most involved) hover around ten or a dozen. The Oakland chapter of AK Press has nine people earning some or all of their living through their work there. Is it only possible, then, to institutionalize equality on a small scale and at the margins of a capitalist system? Or is it possible to create a broader institutionalization of equality? We recall that for Rancière, at least on one reading, there can never be a utopia of equality, but there can be egalitarian collectives that have what I term an institutional character.

There are, in fact, two different questions we might ask here. One is the question of whether indeed it is impossible to have an egalitarian utopia. As we saw, we might ask that question theoretically or empirically. If we lay aside the theoretical approach, as I argued above that we should, this question bleeds into the second one: how far might egalitarian institutions reach? We might be empirically skeptical of the possibility of creating an entire society grounded in the presupposition of equality. But there is a lot of room between small institutions like the co-op and AK Press and an entire society. How far might the institutionalization of equality extend? Is there some point at which the presupposition of equality seems to get lost in the administrative working of an institution?

The other question concerns the process of an egalitarian institution. What kinds of processes must be in place for an institution to presuppose the equality of each of its participants? If decisions are made by voting, does this presuppose the inequality of those who find themselves in the minority? Alternatively, if one utilizes a consensus model, where everyone must agree on a decision, and one person refuses to consent to a decision, does this presuppose the inequality of everyone else?

These two questions become more intertwined as the institutions become larger. In smaller institutions, the questions like those of voting versus consensus don't seem as urgent. In the co-op, for example, people seemed willing either to defer to people who had expertise or to go along with what a majority seemed to favor, unless they had particular reservations with the proposed decisions. With AK Press, as we have seen, everyone is an active participant in the decisions taken by the collective, with conflicts being resolved through voting. But once the institutions become larger, and people no longer know one another or have a circumscribed interest, then it becomes more difficult to resolve the question of how one is to proceed in such a way that respects the presupposition of equality.

These two questions have preoccupied the anarchist tradition. This should be unsurprising, because of anarchism's embrace of radical equality and its rejection of any form of avant-gardism. Among the models proposed to resolve these questions, probably that of what anarchists call *federalism* has been the most common. Its history can be traced back to the early anarchist Pierre-Joseph Proudhon, whose view is summed by the historian of anarchism George Woodcock this way: "The organization of administration should begin locally and as near the direct control of the people as possible; individuals should start the process by federating into communes and associations. Above that primary level the confederal organization would become less an organ of administration than of co-ordination between local units."[10] Federalism can work by either voting or consensus, but has been considered mostly on the consensus model. A federalist organization is formed through a collection of smaller groups that can operate on a face-to-face basis. When confronted with an issue or question, the smaller groups come to a decision independently of one another. Then each of the groups sends a representative to a meeting. (If the organization is very large, this process can be repeated again.) The meeting of representatives seeks a consensus based upon the views of the constituent groups. What is crucial here is that those representatives have no power other than what is sometimes called *administrative* (or in Woodcock's term *co-ordinative*) power. They cannot make any decisions on their own, but must always reflect the views of the groups they are representing. If, at a higher-level meeting, there can be no consensus as to how to act, the representatives return to the lower-level constituent groups, report what has happened, and the process starts again.

There are a number of difficulties that one might raise to this model. One, of course, concerns practicality. Faced with a decision of any complexity, this is a cumbersome mode of operation. It might take a very long time to come to a decision, and in fact it might well be impossible, particularly if there are conflicting interests between constituent groups. Another problem is whether one can really distinguish administrative power from political power among the representatives. Again, faced with an issue of any complexity, the representative must reflect the nuances of group discussion or decision. When does an interpretation of those nuances pass over into the views of the representative himself or herself?

It is difficult to say how these problems might be resolved in a federalist organization. This is because of the paucity of models of large-scale anarchist organizations. The largest scale on which federalism was tried is was the Spanish anarchist movement of the late 1800s and early 1900s. This movement was beset throughout its history, however, by external opposition from both the conservative authorities and communists as well as its own internal divisions.[11]

At least one recent thinker has argued that the problem with much anarchist thinking in this direction is that it makes a fetish of the idea of process. Mark Lance disputes that the issue of equality will be resolved purely by finding the right process.[12] We have seen that neither voting nor consensus is necessarily the preferred model of respecting the equality of participants. Lance argues that it is not simply the process that needs attending to, but the participants in the process itself. They must develop the kinds of skills that would lead to cooperative deliberation and a recognition and acceptance of other viewpoints. Invoking the thought of Aristotle, Lance says that participants in a process of decision-making must cultivate particular virtues, those that will allow them to contribute to a thriving community of equals.

This argument opens out onto a wider question: to what extent can the presupposition of equality be fostered and developed within our current ideological context? One way to read Lance's argument is that educating people toward a particular orientation toward others with a particular set of values is a necessary element of developing institutions of equality. Moreover, this orientation and these values are not characteristic of our own society, one that privileges competition, individualism, and inequality over cooperation, community, and equality. It will be difficult, following Lance's lead, to develop larger-scale institutions of equality (or widespread smaller-scale institutions of equality) until a personal orientation away from current values and toward others can first be developed.

This does not mean that there is no place for small-scale institutions of equality. Those institutions can themselves be educational. They provide models of cooperation that can not only inspire but actually teach through their example the kinds of participation necessary for broadening the scale of a democratic politics. What it does mean is that the challenge of developing these larger institutions is not simply procedural. Resisting hierarchy is not solely a matter of developing processes that favor equality. It goes not only to our institutions but to who we are, to our historically molded identities. Resisting the police orders that govern us must arise not only at the institutional but also at the personal level. This, of course, is a lesson that arises not only from Lance's argument but also from the writings of feminists and thinkers like Michel Foucault, who have shown in various ways that our participation in oppressive political arrangements emerges in part from who we have been taught to be.

The line of thought we are following here would help explain why it is that we have come to accept so many inequalities, so much hierarchy, in our current political context. It would also introduce a note of sobriety into our hope for broadening the presupposition of equality among our institutions. Our struggle is not only against those who benefit from inequality but also, in part, against ourselves and those who suffer inequality. We know that our political world is built on hierarchy, and this line of thought offers at least one explanation why. We need not entirely accept it, however, to recognize that institutions of equality are rare among us and are difficult to maintain.

All of which leaves us with a certain empirical skepticism about how far one might spread the presupposition of equality institutionally. We should note, however, that this skepticism is, in the terms we introduced at the outset of this chapter, empirical rather than theoretical. This is an important distinction for proceeding politically. If the bar to widespread institutionalizing of equality were theoretical, it would be a task without possibility of success. The response to the question of how far one can institutionalize the presupposition of equality would necessarily be: not at all. But the more empirical skepticism (or sobriety, if one prefers) that we have offered here does not lay claim to any in-principle answer to that question. Confronted with the question of how far one can institutionalize the presupposition of equality, the answer is: we don't know. We see many obstacles to its widespread development, but we also recognize that history is contingent and changeable.

This way of thinking about things places us in a position that is between utopian naïveté and cynical despair. That, it seems to me, is the right place to be. Utopianism is often misplaced and, if the twentieth century is to be a guide, more than a little dangerous. Cynical despair, of course, gets us nowhere. It is also empirically suspect, as successful movements of equality have shown. We must proceed with sober hope, building upon and cultivating the presupposition of equality when and where the openings for it present themselves. This way of proceeding offers no guarantees. But just as it offers no guarantees of success, it offers no guarantees of failure. We have seen here, in at least two cases, long-term projects of institutional equality that have sustained themselves in a society of inequality. As for where our projects of equality might go from here, we turn to that question in the final chapter.

Notes

I would like to thank the Upstate Food Co-op and AK Press for allowing me to talk with several of their members about how these institutions operate and for allowing me to sit in on meetings. This generosity should not be mistaken for agreement by my various hosts with the positions espoused here. Although I told folks the perspective of this book project, I did not ask them whether they agreed with any of it. And, as I mention in the text, I'm sure there are people I spoke with who would not embrace the Rancièrean perspective.

1 Bakunin, Michael, *Statism and Anarchy*, tr. Marshall Shatz, Cambridge: Cambridge University Press, 1990, p. 137.
2 *On the Shores of Politics*, p. 84.
3 May, Todd, Noys, Benjamin, and Newman, Saul, "Democracy, anarchism, and radical politics today: An Interview with Jacques Rancière," tr. John Lechte, *Anarchist Studies*, vol. 16, no. 2, 2008, p. 173.
4 "Ten Theses on Politics."
5 My central source for the history of the co-op is an as-yet unpublished paper by Richard Ogwala-Omara, Rita McMillan, and Kenneth Robinson, "A Co-operative Surviving with Volunteer Workers: A Case of the Upstate Food Coop, South Carolina." I am grateful to Richard Ogwala-Omara for sharing this paper with me, as well as generously offering time for an interview during my research on the co-op.
6 On a related note, Rancière's politics does not recognize a particular place for animal rights. This is not to say that he denies animal rights. What he is interested in is a democratic politics, a participatory politics. This is why, as we have seen, he grounds his politics in the equality of *speaking* beings. The question of the rights of or obligations to non-human animals is distinct from the question of a democratic politics, neither militated for or against by such a politics.
7 For a remarkable account of the food supplied by fast food chains, see Michael Pollan's *The Omnivore's Dilemma*, New York: Penguin Press, 2006. He traces the origins of four meals, the first of which is a fast

food meal, which he shows to be a disaster for the food, the environment, and the consumer.

8 This was the situation when I visited the press in March 2009.

9 Here they are: (1) All collective members have equal decision-making power (we each get one vote on all decisions affecting the collective); (2) Every collective member makes the same wage; (3) We enter with nothing and leave with nothing; there will be no owners or investors; (4) The Statement of Purpose and by-laws can only be amended by a unanimous vote of all collective members; (5) If AK Press ceases to exist, its assets, after repaying all debts, will go to a project with a similar Statement of Purpose.

10 Woodcock, George, *Anarchism: A History of Libertarian Ideas and Movements*, Cleveland: The World Publishing Co., 1962, pp. 140–1. For more on Proudhon's federalism, and the history of the anarchist movement generally, see also James Joll's *The Anarchists*, 2nd edn, Cambridge, MA: Harvard University Press, 1979, esp. pp. 59–61.

11 For a sensitive history of the Spanish anarchist movement, see Murray Bookchin's *The Spanish Anarchists: The Heroic Years 1868–1936*, New York: Free Life Editions, 1977.

12 Lance, Mark, "Fetishizing Process," http://homepage.mac.com/abuemma/.Public/activist percent20stuff/fetishizing percent20process. doc.

6

Democratic Politics Now

> The principle of equality is the revolutionary principle, not only
> because it challenges hierarchies, but because it asserts that all men
> are equally whole. And the converse is just as true: to accept inequal-
> ity as natural is to become fragmented, is to see oneself as no more
> than the sum of a set of capacities and needs.
>
> John Berger[1]

We come now to the question that has driven this book. It is a question that haunts our time. What, if any, possibilities are there for a
democratic politics? In an age of dispersed globalization, where can
our hope for democratic movements lie? How can we create them, or
at least, where and how can they be created? In short, can there be a
democratic politics in the time in which we live?

It may seem that we have already answered these questions, insofar
as they can be answered. Can there be a democratic politics? Yes. We
have seen examples of it. We have seen it in Montréal, Palestine,
southern Mexico, South Carolina, and Oakland, California. We
have seen it in diverse forms and under diverse circumstances. We
may not be able to glean from these examples the key to organizing
democratic movements. However, there really isn't a key. We probably all know this. If there had been a Holy Grail for those who seek
to organize alongside the part that has no part, it would have long
ago been found. After all, people have been oppressed in all societies
and across a variety of registers for so long, if there had been some
trick to getting those without a part to realize and to act upon their
own equality, somebody would have figured it out over the past
thousands of years.

This is not to say that there are no lessons to be culled from these
examples. There are. We need to draw some threads from among them;
and in a bit, we will. However, the questions in the first paragraph of
this chapter do not lie exactly there. They do not ask simply out of a
desire to know, in order better to understand and perhaps to engage
in social change. For many who ask themselves and one another the

questions in that paragraph, it is really the last question that matters. And the reason it matters is that there is a sense, the examples of this book notwithstanding, that the answer is in the negative.

For those with this sense, the examples here are marginal activities swimming against a strong current. The two large-scale democratic movements are the first Palestinian intifada and the Zapatista movement. However, the first intifada faded over a decade ago, and has been replaced by something less democratic. And the Zapatista movement is hardly in a healthy condition at this moment, the victim of the low-intensity warfare of the Mexican state.

One might point to other examples of resistance, even if not all of these are as democratic as the examples cited in this book. There is struggle against oppression in Chechnya, Burma, Haiti, and elsewhere. Immigrants in the US and elsewhere are protesting their situation and the attitudes against them. In perhaps the largest movement, environmental degradation is being addressed across a variety of fronts, and those who cause it are beginning to be confronted. Those who have a part are meeting resistance on a variety of fronts from those who have not and from their supporters. While these movements may not all presuppose equality, there is at least a demand for equality, even if inchoate, that animates many of them. (There are, of course, other resistance movements as well, such as those animated by religious fervor of one sort or another, which are not cause for hope and will not be addressed outside the parentheses of this sentence.)

However, among many of us, these examples still do not address the sense of hopelessness that suffuses progressive politics. One acknowledges these movements, but still feels as though something central, the democratic dream, is losing sway. These movements feel to many like puddles in a very parched land. They are, to be sure, worth supporting. But, in the heat of our time, they seem ready to evaporate without a trace.

Perhaps the problem is not so much with the movements themselves, but with how we view them. The left has a revolutionary tradition, a tradition that stems from the Marxist view that sees history producing periodic wholesale changes. This is one of the central themes that seems to distinguish the left from liberalism. Liberals embrace reform and worry about revolution. Leftists or progressives embrace revolution and are leery of reform. If change isn't revolutionary, then the suspicion is that it isn't really change. It's just a form of co-optation.

The idea of revolution is inseparable from that of utopia, an idea that we considered briefly in the previous chapter. The connection is clear: revolutionary change ushers in a completely different society. Where there is now oppression, alienation, and disenfranchisement, after the revolution there will be equality, meaningfulness, and solidarity. Again the distinction with liberalism is apt. Liberals reject utopia, seeing in it a dangerous illusion. Leftists embrace utopia, seeing in it a sign of hope.

There are many folks I've met on the left, although they are by no means the majority, who are both revolutionary and utopian. I believe there is good reason, however, to reject both ideas. A full discussion would take us beyond the concerns of this chapter, but it is probably worth gesturing at here. We can divide revolutionary thought broadly into two types, which we might call qualitative and quantitative. Qualitative revolutionary thought takes it that the key to revolutionary change lies at a particular point in the social order. If one changes that point – the Archimedean point of political change – the rest of the social order will change of its own accord. Traditional Marxism is a theory of qualitative revolution. Change the economic structure and the rest of society will follow.

There is little to say at this historical moment in defense of qualitative revolutionary thought, since the twentieth century might be read as its refutation. As Michel Foucault once said in response to a question about the future of resistance, "I think that to imagine another system is to extend our participation in the present system. This is perhaps what happened in the history of the Soviet Union: apparently, new institutions were in fact based on elements taken from an earlier system – the Red Army reconstituted on the model of the Czarist army, the return to realism in art, and the emphasis on traditional family morality."[2]

Quantitative revolutionary thought is different. It does not seek an Archimedean point for change. It recognizes that the different oppressions of a society – economic, familial, political, racial, sexual, etc. – are irreducible to a single site that produces and explains them all. These oppressions may be related, but they are not reducible. Often, one hears a critique of capitalism that uses the term *capitalism* not just as an economic system but as an entire economic, social, and political order. That would be indicative of a quantitative approach to revolution. The idea here is that all of the various oppressions must be changed in order for a utopia to arise. Much traditional anarchist thought is oriented toward quantitative revolutionary change.

Quantitative revolutionary change is more sober and, for that reason, more promising than its qualitative cousin. It does not hold the illusion that liberation comes from struggle at a single site. It recognizes that struggle must be had across a variety of fronts in order for a utopia to arise. What makes it revolutionary, however, is the belief that a utopia is possible, that a massive social change can occur in which all oppressions are overthrown and a final liberation achieved.

What distinguishes Rancière's thought from that of a quantitative revolutionary? Of course, he himself is nothing if not sober. He believes that politics is rare, as we have seen. "[P]olitics doesn't always happen – it actually happens very little or rarely." Moreover, as we have also seen, he does not believe that it can be institutionalized, at least on a large scale. But suppose we took it that Rancière's thought would allow for the institutionalization, at least at a local level, of democracy. Would we then be on the first step toward quantitative revolutionary change?

Not necessarily. There may or may not be enough local and intersecting changes to bring about a change momentous enough to be called revolutionary. More to the point, though, the quantitative view of revolution is probably best prised apart from the idea of revolution altogether, or at least from the distinction between reform and revolution. When, exactly (or even roughly) does a quantitative change become revolutionary instead of just reformist? How many different changes, in how many different locales, across how many different practices, before one can say that a society has moved from reform to revolution? If we are to think of democracy as building from the bottom up, and recognize that there is no Archimedean point for revolutionary change, perhaps it is best to give up talk of revolution and reform altogether. Democratic movements, when they mobilize an obligation to hear, introduce changes into the societies within which they take place. Some of those changes are smaller, some larger. In some cases, we might look back and say that a certain change or set of changes amounted to a revolution. But that is neither here nor there for thinking about a democratic politics. The distinction between reform and revolution as a distinction between liberal and left orientation is not, to my mind, a helpful one. It is best abandoned.

If we abandon discussion of revolution as opposed to reform, then would this mitigate the sense I described above of hopelessness or malaise regarding progressive political change? After all, if what we're seeking is no longer a total social change that would merit the title *revolutionary*, can we not just be satisfied with the political changes and resistance movements that are with us today, or others that we can create? If we give up false or misplaced hopes does that not leave us with the real ones, real ones that now shine brighter because they do not suffer in comparison with the false ones?

That would be too quick. The distinction between reform and revolution has played an important role in the left's view of itself, and the loss of revolutionary hope in the post-Marxist period has taken its toll on the left. However, that is not all that is in play in the devastation the left now feels. There is something else going on, something that has to do with globalization. It has put a strain on progressive political action. This other thing – and there may be still others as well – has many leftists feeling at a loss about how to think about politics and about how to create or support democratic political movements. It has also, and perhaps more profoundly, given rise to the suspicion that, in the end, progressive politics is largely dead, or at least defunct in our time.

We can approach this other thing by pausing to consider an analysis of the movements of poor people given by Frances Fox Piven and Richard Cloward. Piven and Cloward have devoted their lives to studying movements of people without material resources. Although we have not been concerned entirely with political movements among the impoverished here, and although the victims of neoliberal globalization are not only the impoverished, the focus Piven and Cloward place on poor people's movements are useful for understanding our own situation. This is for two reasons. First, in the neoliberal capitalist order, among the parts that have no part is importantly the part that is impoverished by the operation of that order. Second, several of their insights can be understood as applying to mass movements that are not solely anchored among the impoverished.

In their book, *Poor People's Movements: Why They Succeed, How They Fail*, they offer an overview of the dynamic of political change in such movements. They argue against the view that poor people's political resistance always arises in periods of general economic change, largely because economic change is always happening, and often not to the benefit of the poor. It is not the fact of change, then, but the magnitude and speed of change that are the relevant factors. "[P]rotest movements do not arise during ordinary periods; they arise when large-scale changes undermine political stability."[3] Their models for these periods of large-scale changes are both in the

US, their object of study: the 1930s, during the Great Depression, and the 1960s, in the wake of massive economic change in the South and consequent migration of African Americans to the North. During both these periods, massive economic displacement led to resistance against the current order. But, "since periods of profound social dislocations are infrequent, so too are opportunities for protest among the lower classes."[4] Politics among the poor is, as Rancière would say, rare.

Moreover, as Piven and Cloward note, resistance is not directed against the roots of displacement or dislocation – i.e. the structure and operation of the social, political, and economic system – but rather against the specific situations in which people find themselves. "Workers experience the factory, the speeding rhythm of the assembly line, the foreman, the spies and the guards . . . They do not experience monopoly capitalism. People on relief experience the shabby waiting rooms, the overseer or the caseworker, and the dole. They do not experience American social welfare policy."[5] Thus, resistance tends to be local and concrete rather than general and abstract. The social order is not confronted, only particular manifestations of it in particular places.

One can see how the resistance of the 1930s and the 1960s might have operated on the model they provide. To take the example of the civil rights movement of the 1960s, the dislocation of African Americans during the economic modernization of the South disrupted the way of life of African Americans, who until then had lived in a largely feudal system. This system was not benign. But it was stable. When it began to disintegrate, this opened the door for resistance movements. These movements, in turn, could be directed against local targets of dissatisfaction: the bus driver who ushered African Americans to the back of the bus, the restaurant owner who wouldn't serve them, the police who wouldn't protect them, the voting official who refused to register them.

We can put this point in Rancièrean terms. African Americans acting on the presupposition of their equality came into immediate conflict at a local level with those who reinforced the police order. That is why the civil rights movement, seen as a struggle against an entire system of oppression, is inseparable from the civil rights movement as a set of local struggles against particular targets. The systematic oppression of African Americans, particularly but not solely in the South, was a system of structured hierarchies that were enacted in face-to-face encounters. To challenge the presupposition of inequality that structured those encounters was to challenge the system itself. Although the US civil rights movement of the 1960s was certainly a struggle against racism, to describe it solely in that way risks missing the local nature of resistance to which Piven and Cloward have called our attention.

Much the same can be said of the anti-Vietnam war movement of the same period. The anti-war movement was not a poor people's movement. But one of the key sources of its motivation, as we can see in comparison with the 2003 US invasion of Iraq, was local in nature: the draft. Without the draft, the larger issues of the unjust character of the war and role of US imperialism have trouble finding traction.

We can relate these ideas drawn from Piven and Cloward to the situation of globalization today. Globalization, at least in its neoliberal guise of corporate hegemony, is a massively dislocating force for many of the world's poor. One study notes that in the period between 1995 and 2002, "the real average GDP per capita of the 'non-advanced countries' comprising four-fifths of the world's population, has fallen absolutely, from $1400 to $1100 per year."[6] Another study notes that "Between 1960 and 1994 the gap in per capita income between the richest fifth of the world's people (most in developed countries) and the poorest fifth (most in developing countries) more than doubled – from 30:1 to 78:1. By the mid-1990s this trend was becoming more marked: by 1995 the ratio was 82:1."[7] The author goes on to note that "In Latin America, long regarded as a relatively advanced region, the number of people living in poverty increased between 1990 and 1995 from 183 million to 230 million, or 48 percent of the continent's population."[8]

These massive dislocations are reinforced by the neoliberal policies of the International Monetary Fund and the World Bank. By insisting on the primacy of debt repayments to first world banks, privatization, cutting public budgets, and deregulation, these bodies pressure developing countries to shift their wealth both to developed countries and to the wealthier segments of their own population.[9] Economist Ha-Joon Chang points out that, "Since the 1980s . . . when the continent embraced neo-liberalism, Latin American has been growing at less than one-third of the rate of the 'bad old days.' Even if we discount the 1980s as a decade of adjustment and take it out of the equation, *per capita* income in the region during the 1990s grew at basically half the rate of the 'bad old days' (3.1% vs. 1.7 %) . . . As for Africa . . . the region has seen a *fall* in living standards."[10]

These would seem to be propitious conditions for a poor people's movement, or for several of them. And, in fact, there has been resistance, most notably in South America. In recent years, governments of the left have begun to re-emerge in South America as the fruits of globalization are being harvested there. At the time of this writing, Venezuela, Ecuador, and Bolivia, and to some extent Brazil all have governments critical of the effects of globalization.

In addition, one of the movements we have studied here, that of the Zapatistas, is directly critical of the dislocations caused by the neoliberal orientation of globalization. The Zapatistas, and Subcommandante Marcos, have consistently recognized the effects of neoliberal globalization on the indigenous populations of southern Mexico. The changes to Article 27 of the Mexican Constitution, discussed in Chapter 4, are a result of the pressure globalization has placed to privatize land worked by Mexico's campesinos.

However, these movements seem to lack proportion relative to their cause. First, they are geographically confined. Although the effects of neoliberal globalization are, precisely, global, the resistance movements are largely centered in Central and South America. Second, aside from the Zapatistas, these movements have been expressed largely through electoral rather than grassroots means. This is not to say that there have been no popular expressions of discontent. For instance, the riots in Bolivia after the US corporation Bechtel took over Bolivia's water supply (riots that set the stage for the election of Evo Morales) were certainly a spontaneous movement from below. However, these expressions have not given rise to democratic movements of the kind described in this book.

Third, the one movement that did take hold, the Zapatista movement, has not been able to sustain itself. Although it received support and sympathy from outside Mexico, and although its analyses of our current situation remain trenchant, the Zapatistas have struggled to maintain their movement and to bring concrete gains to the people of Chiapas and elsewhere. The causes of this failure are in part due to the low-intensity warfare waged against the indigenous people by the Mexican government. One suspects, however, and this, I believe, is the getting to the core of the issue, that something else is also involved.

Piven and Cloward's approach to poor people's movements claims that they arise during periods of massive dislocation. We have seen here that such dislocation is characteristic of neoliberal globalization. However, they also insist that resistance tends to be directed toward local targets. It is not monopoly capitalism or American social policy that is rebelled against. Instead, resistance is directed instead against those within the experience of the oppressed. This is not to say that there are no demonstrations against policies and laws (although demonstrations against neoliberal capitalism itself are more rare). It is to say, though, that in order for a movement to take place there must be a local hook on which to hang resistance. In other words, in addition to massive dislocation, there must be local sites that become the immediate target of discontent. Even if those local sites are not the primary causes of the problem, they provide a way to begin to establish publicly that there is indeed a problem. One can see demonstrations against police abuse in minority communities this way. The demonstrations are often prompted by single acts of violence, but they quickly begin to address larger issues of community marginalization.[11]

And here is where the difficulty lies. With neoliberal globalization, it is difficult to find a hook. There are plenty of local effects, but the particular adversary to address goes missing. It is of the character of transnational capitalism that the source of economic oppression is often thousands of miles away, separated from those it exploits by many levels of bureaucracy, language, and national borders.

Compare this situation with, for instance, the US civil rights movement. There the adversary was easy to identity. The white power structure in the South was local, and African Americans could easily see who benefited from their oppression. Moreover, and this is also crucial for our own day, for those who came to support the civil rights movement in the North, images of oppression were stark and available. Northerners watched the resistance of African Americans and their treatment at the hands of the likes of Birmingham sheriff Bull Connor. This prompted both identification with the presupposed equality of those who struggled and anger at those who denied that equality. This in its turn prompted support and solidarity.

In the current neoliberal environment, both the local hooks and the media images are missing. The loss of media images is easy to explain. First, a clear denial of equality of the type exemplified in the US civil rights movement generates images. Those images are usually of a confrontation between oppressor and oppressed. There are no analogous images of neoliberal oppression. This is not only because it is difficult to have access to private companies operating in the third world – although that fact is not negligible. It is also because those images would only show people working under difficult conditions.

That doesn't prompt the kind of identification and anger that starker images of oppression do.

As for the local hooks, it would seem that they do exist. After all, neoliberalism's operation in the third world certainly has, as Piven and Cloward put it, "the factory, the speeding rhythm of the assembly line, the foreman, the spies and the guards." Aren't these the proper local objects of resistance? Moreover, haven't there been horror stories of, for example, Nike's treatment of female workers in its factories, just the kind of stories that prompt both resistance and solidarity? Doesn't this, at least, provide the combination of rapid economic dislocation and particular targets that Piven and Cloward argue are necessary for struggle to occur?

In fact, struggle does occur. There are attempts at unionization, outbreaks of spontaneous resistance, and a brewing discontent and resentment. But what seems to be missing is the kind of mass resistance that would merit the name of a movement. And here, I want to suggest that among the missing elements is precisely the difficulty of articulating the presupposition of equality, of finding the point where economic dislocation can be turned into a democratic politics.

There is a tendency to view economics as separate from politics. This is a capitalist view. On this view, political democracy is compatible with economic hierarchy. One can exercise all the rights of a citizen, equal to anyone else, and yet be subject to hierarchical treatment at work, and this is not a problem. There is, of course, no lack of justifications offered for this distinction, from the sanctity of private property to the efficiency of the market. What we must recognize, however, is how the two – economy and politics – have been separated.

One result of this separation is that economic demands are often thought of as distinct from political demands. While the latter may concern issues like equality, the former are simply material. People want a better standard of living, so they strike or negotiate or slow down the workplace or, failing that, look for another job. Economic demands, then, are material and individual, while political demands are principled and collective.

To embrace Rancière's view is to reject the necessity of this separation. Economic demands can indeed be principled and collective. They can indeed concern the question of equality, because in the economic realm, as in the traditional political realm, equality and hierarchy are at stake. This does not mean that *all* economic demands are principled and collective, or, to put the point in terms we have been employing, that all demands stem from a democratic politics. With economic struggle, as with other types of struggle, "Equality is not a given that politics then presses into service, an essence embodied in the law or a goal politics sets itself the task of attaining. It is a mere assumption that needs to be discerned within the practices implementing it."[12] With economic struggle, as with other struggle, one must discern whether the presupposition of equality is operating or whether there are only other motives, such as material comfort. (This does not mean, of course, that other motives cannot be present in a democratic political struggle. The question is the existence of the presupposition of equality, not the non-existence of other elements.)

My suggestion here is that we must add, in addition to Piven and Cloward's elements of poor people's struggles, at least one more: the operation of the presupposition of equality. Piven and Cloward have offered important conditions for a poor people's movement, but have neglected the spark of the movement itself, the conditions under which one moves from a situation ready for struggle to a movement. This, I believe, must involve the decision, even when it is not explicitly stated but only implicitly acted, that equality is at stake.

To put the point another way, the conditions Piven and Cloward address for poor people's movements – rapid social dislocation and a local target – do not automatically cause those movements. Even under those conditions, it is not necessary that poor people's movements will arise. Undoubtedly, they would agree. Then what else is necessary in order for there to be a movement? One of those things is a decision by the people themselves to act. That decision, inasmuch as it is a democratic one, is a decision to act from the presupposition of equality.

There is something irreducible about this decision. By that I mean that one cannot set up or recognize a particular set of social conditions and conclude definitively that a resistance movement will emerge. People have to decide to act. Events that, in retrospect, seem to be precipitants of movements (e.g. Rosa Parks' refusal to sit at the back of the bus in Montgomery in 1955), only become precipitants precisely in retrospect, after people have decided to mobilize. There were other African Americans who refused to give up their seats in Southern buses before her, even during the period of upheaval for Southern African Americans of the 1950s. Her act was no different, except that it assumed a different significance after people decided to act collectively from the presupposition of their equality.

This is not to deny that particular social conditions or external events are important. The ones Piven and Cloward cite for poor people's movement do seem significant. The existence of a draft was a crucial element of resistance to the Vietnam war. Rather, the claim is that something must come from below, a collective decision made to act by the part that has no part, in order for a democratic resistance movement to arise.

One might ask, in passing, whether the decision to act out of the presupposition of equality is enough by itself to create a social movement. That is, can the democratic moment of decision occur *regardless* of social conditions? After all, poor people's movements are just one type of movement. We have seen others in this book. Is it possible for a democratic movement to arise without there having to be necessitating or founding conditions?

My suspicion is that the answer to that question is no. Something has to motivate a movement. History does not, to my knowledge, provide examples of people's forming democratic movements without some kind of motivation (even if that motivation is, as initially with the local food co-op, the desire for cheaper food). Once a movement starts, it can perhaps develop into an institutionalized form, as we have seen. But movements start in reaction to and under specific social, political, and/or economic conditions. As Rancière would say, democracy starts always as a dissensus. Although, as we have seen in the previous chapter, there are questions one could raise regarding whether democracy must always remain a dissensus as well as whether the dissensus is direct or indirect, it is difficult to imagine that it would start any other way.

This brings us back to the question we asked a few pages back. Why is it that, given the dislocations neoliberal globalization is causing, there are not more poor people's movements? One answer we gave was that neoliberalism does not provide a set of images to motivate resistance and struggle. This cannot be all, however. There were democratic struggles before there were media to provide images of them. The reflections we have engaged in here bring us to another answer: the difficulty of seeing struggles through the lens of the presupposition of equality. And this difficulty itself seems to stem from at least two related causes. The first is a certain lack of connection between the local targets or hooks and the sites of the problem itself. The second is what we might call the economization of political struggle.

We have seen that there is, in a sense, a set of local hooks or targets. There are overseers and factories and police. However, there is a disconnect between these overseers and factories and police on the one side and the owners and directors on the other. In earlier struggles, particularly in the economic sphere, overseers and managers were not far removed from the owners and directors of the companies they represented. With neoliberal globalization it is more difficult to see the owner in the manager, because the owner likely lives on another continent, speaks another language, and is immersed in a different culture. This means that struggle against the overseer or manager remains a local affair. It is mediated by local authorities and resolved at the local level. Under these conditions, it becomes difficult for resistance to grow into a mass movement.

Piven and Cloward comment that, "people cannot defy institutions to which they have no access, and to which they make no contribution."[13] The feeling of a lack of access is characteristic of neoliberal globalization. Struggle as one might, the ultimate target of one's struggle seems hopelessly distant. This does not imply, to be sure, that there cannot be local resistance. There can be, and, as we have documented throughout this book, there is local struggle. The difficulty is in the leap from local struggle to a mass movement. While the misnamed "anti-globalization" movement was an attempt to create this mass movement, and while the Zapatistas have called attention to the global implications of their struggle, no sustained movement has yet arisen that successfully connects local struggles to one another and weaves the threads among them. If this is to happen, the presupposition of the equality of anyone and everyone will have to be a central element of the framework.

The second cause – or better, motivation, since we want to deny any strict causality here – is the economization of political struggle. We noted above the capitalist tendency to separate economics from politics. Economic struggles do not concern equality; only political struggle is about equality. If this is so, then in a world of neoliberal globalization almost no struggle can be about equality. Struggles are about economics: better wages or living conditions or work environments. In short, struggles are about better lives, not equality.

The economization of politics has not only affected third world countries. Rancière recognizes that it is also a European phenomenon. The elites of Europe cannot understand why, for instance, many Europeans are leery of the European Union or the economic integration of Europe. Their (often diverse and conflicting) political concerns are interpreted as economic ones. He writes, "it is more difficult to demonstrate that the free circulation of capital demanding an ever more rapid profitability is a providential law that shall lead humanity to a better future. Faith is required. The 'ignorance' that people are being reproached for is simply its lack of faith."[14] When global leaders and the mainstream media look upon resistance, they do not see assertions of equality. They see demands for participation in the consumerist world in which they are invested and through which they see others.

To the extent that such a view takes hold, it salts the ground of democratic politics. This is for two reasons. First, if economics is never a matter of equality, but instead a matter of living standards, then the concept of equality itself is marginalized. People do not consider equality to be a stake in struggle, simply because they do not consider equality at all. If equality is nothing more than the ability to vote and to buy goods, then equality is no longer a stake in most struggles. It is simply a matter of getting by with a little more.

Following from this, if equality is no longer a stake in struggle, then neither is collective action. What binds together a collectivity into a democratic political subjectivity, as we have seen, is the presupposition of equality. Once that presupposition goes by the board, so goes the motivation for solidarity. It's not that there cannot be collective struggle. There can. However, this struggle is not a solidarity among those who presuppose their common equality. It is an alliance among those whose individual interests find a temporary convergence. Under these conditions, movements are difficult to build. A mass movement requires solidarity among its members, a sense of commonality in their immersion in struggle and resistance. This commonality does not require that everyone be the same, but that everyone sees himself or herself in connection with others. The position of this book, drawn from Rancière's thought, is that that connection largely runs through the presupposition of equality. Once that presupposition goes missing, so does the solidarity that stems from it.

It is not that nobody feels any solidarity, or that there aren't local struggles. Rather, the problem is that there isn't the glue that binds people together into a larger democratic mass movement. Also, the point is not that there aren't mass movements. Religious fundamentalism, to which we will return momentarily, is nothing if not a mass movement. What we do not see are *democratic* mass movements, mass movements that presuppose the equality of every speaking being.

Again, to emphasize the point, my claim is not that economics has replaced politics on the neoliberal stage. This would itself be too neoliberal a claim. Rather, I'm suggesting that there is an insistence within current discourse upon the separation between economics and politics itself, a separation that seeks to withdraw political stakes – i.e. the presupposition of equality – from the economic realm and from economic struggle. In this sense, it is worth preserving an aspect of the Marxist tradition. For Marxism, at least when it sheds its elements of economic determinism, economics has never been separate from politics. All economic struggles have political stakes. Those who rule and those who benefit economically are, while not always the same people, at least in league with each other. Challenges to the economic order can (although they don't always and necessarily) constitute challenges to the hierarchical order of society. The loss of this recognition and the replacement of a political consciousness with a solely economic one blunts the force of all resistance.

It appears to many that, rather than economic struggles having political stakes, the situation is the opposite. Challenges to hierarchy and assertions of authority are simply economic demands in disguise. What people want, it is argued, is a comfortable life. Equality does not matter. Therefore, where equality is asserted one must look behind the assertion for the comfort that is really being sought. This view is in keeping with neoliberal globalization, and supports policies that keep it in power. Political issues are turned into technological ones. The question of who has say over what aspects of people's lives is turned into a question of how best to run the economic order. There may be differences among elites regarding how to answer that question. For committed neoliberals, the answer is to allow the free market to decide everything. In Europe, among those who support the European Union, the answer is different. There needs to be more direction from above and a greater commitment to fair working conditions and unemployment compensation, even at the cost of greater government intervention. What both sides agree on, however, is that there are no political issues – no issues of hierarchy and equality. There are only economic ones.

Rancière sums up this situation in a dense but precise passage. The task of contemporary politics is

> the political reduction of the social (that is to say the distribution of wealth) and the social reduction of the political (that is to say the distribution of various powers and the imaginary investments attached to them). On the one hand, to quiet the conflict of rich and poor through the distribution of rights, responsibilities and controls; on the other, to quiet the passions aroused by the occupation of the centre by virtue of spontaneous social activities.[15]

Politics assigns proper places and limits to economic activity; the social offers economic incentives to calm any discontent about the hierarchical police order. From both sides, though, the project is the same: to quiet.

This is one source – I think it is the primary source – of current despair over the lack of resistance to neoliberal globalization, and to current egregious policies by the US and others more generally. Although there is much to protest, and there is much dislocation caused by the neoliberal order, the stakes of democracy have been marginalized. Because of the global dispersion of targets and the economization of the political, it has become harder to see a way toward a politics of the kind that characterized the civil rights movement in the US, the anti-colonization movements of India or Algeria, or the resistance to Israel's occupation of Palestine that characterized the first intifada. The presupposition of equality, the wellspring of democratic mass movements, has gone missing, and in its place is a more individualistic or tribal self-serving consciousness, one that preserves the current police order even when it sees itself as struggling against it.

In this last connection, we return once again to the issue of identity politics. Although in some ways it has receded from its pride of place in the academic world, identity politics remains alive in the global order, as the rise of Islamic fundamentalism will attest. It has been cast, in the context of neoliberal globalization, as Jihad versus McWorld.[16] The slogan isn't entirely wrong. But why is it Jihad rather than something else that is challenging McWorld?

There can be a variety of different responses to the difficulty of acting from the presupposition of equality. Withdrawal is one, and we have seen no lack of it. The apathy that is ascribed to young people is, I believe, a response to the problems we have canvassed in this chapter. There are those who see apathy as a sort of social disease afflicting people who are plugged into electronic devices and thus removed from concerns about the world in which they live. For the most part, I do not share this view. To me, apathy is not the disease; it is the symptom. The disease is hopelessness, a feeling that one cannot change the world for the better. Piven and Cloward, as we have seen, put it succinctly: *people cannot defy institutions to which they have no access, and to which they make no contribution.* My addition here would be only to insist that, whether or not people have access, neoliberal globalization gives them the sense that they don't. And much of the governance of neoliberalism assures them that they don't. So they take what is on order – consumer goods, if they can afford them – and withdraw.

On the surface, religious fundamentalism seems to take the opposite tack from withdrawal. Rather than pulling back, it fights. Whether in its Islamic form, or in its Christian form in the US, its Hindu form in India, its Jewish form in Israel, or elsewhere, religious fundamentalism confronts neoliberal globalization with a return to essential elements of a particular culture. In this sense, religious fundamentalism is indistinct from other forms of identity politics that have characterized the left. Against the current order, identity politics posits an essence that is to be respected and which asserts itself against the prevailing order. Although there are forms of progressive identity politics that do not operate from the concept of an essence (of blackness, of the feminine, of gayness), almost all identity politics hold a particular element or complex of elements as a source of self-assertion. Non-essentialist identity politics may be ontologically different from essentialist identity politics, but, as a political matter, the two are generally indistinguishable. And, like religious fundamentalism, progressive identity politics poses its identity against the current police order.

Beneath this difference between identity politics – religious or otherwise – and withdrawal, there is an underlying similarity. Identity politics, like withdrawal, is self-absorbed. What counts is not the equality that we all share, but who I am or what I want. Self-concern, whether individual or collective, replaces solidarity.

With the presupposition of equality, who I am is, in an important way, empty. This is what Rancière means when he says that democratic politics does not unify, it declassifies. In some sense, of course, a democratic politics does unify – it does so through subjectification. But it does not unify by way of gathering people under the banner of a particular characteristic they possess. Equality simply means equal intelligence, which itself simply means the ability of each of us to create meaningful lives without the paternalism of a hierarchy. That is how solidarity arises. What matters is not who we are in our peculiarities but simply our equality.

For both withdrawal and identity politics, who one is matters. Or, to be more precise, the questions that motivate one are centered around oneself and/or one's particular qualities. Rather than being equal to others, one privileges one's desires or one's group identity. In the wake of the marginalization of equality, this should not be surprising. In the wake of neoliberal globalization, it could almost be expected. Under a rampant capitalist ethic, one is encouraged to think of oneself first and foremost. This is in keeping with the tradition of Adam Smith's famous dictum: "It is not from the benevolence of the butcher, the brewer, or the baker, that we expect our dinner, but from their regard to their own interest. We address ourselves, not to their humanity but to their self-love."[17] Privileging the self at the expense of the equality of all is encouraged from two sides. From one side, if one privileges one's own needs and desires and works to better oneself, this will bring the greatest utility to society. From the other, it is precisely competition rather than solidarity with the other that is encouraged by capitalism. This means both that one *ought* to treat others as competitors, and that one *might as well* anyway, since they are going to treat one another that way. In both withdrawal and identity politics, one can see these dynamics at work.

Under these conditions, it is not difficult to see the obstacles faced by projects acting under the presupposition of equality. They can seem, as they do to many, to be naïve, anachronistic, out of place. Neoliberal capitalism, driven by a general cynicism about solidarity, undermines the equality that forms its democratic soil. This leads to hopelessness among those for whom solidarity under the banner of equality is the basis of political change. Organizers begin to feel out of touch, and the parts without a part feel reduced to isolation or rage. Absent a democratic politics, Rancière tells us, "there is only the order of domination or the disorder of revolt."[18]

There is, of course, much that might be said about the deleterious effects that the marginalization of equality and solidarity produce. I want to call attention to one more. The self-centeredness of the capitalist ethic opposes not only the embrace of equality as a presupposition, but the nobility of that embrace as a project of politics. By placing one in competition with others, by seeing this competition as the natural order of things, neoliberal globalization undermines the sense that by engaging in a democratic politics, one is becoming immersed in something larger than oneself. The idea that one is ennobled through solidarity with others faces charges of nostalgia or empty self-righteousness.

Many of us in the US will recall the enthusiasm we felt when we watched those who marched for their civil rights or for the civil rights of others, or against the unjust war in Vietnam. Many in Paris will recall the sense that there might be a real liberation on the other side of the events of May 1968. Those in the former Czechoslovakia will recall similar feelings during the Prague Spring, and there are many

Chinese for whom the days before the Tiananmen Square massacre were a glimpse into a future worth having. These enthusiasms are not empty. They draw those who witness them, and even more so those who participate in them, toward a world of hope. They display for all to see the contingency of a current police order, and the possibility of other ways of living together. They do this for no other reason than because they are the actions of people who know themselves to be equal to those in power, and because the hope that animates those actions is contagious.

It is precisely this contagion of hope, this nobility that binds itself to the sense that we are indeed all equal, that the ethic of neoliberal capitalism seeks to extinguish.

Where, then, might our hope lie?

In part, the answer to this question is simple and unsurprising. Our hope lies where it has always lain: in the actions of those who presuppose themselves to be equal to one another. It lies in the demos, and in those who act alongside them. Our hope lies with Algerian immigrants in Montréal, with the Palestinians, with the Zapatistas, with food co-ops and anarchist publishers. It lies with all those about whom we hear little until we attune our ears to the democratic politics that continues to assert itself beneath the capitalist din. When we turn away from the spectacle offered us by our politicians, our public athletes, our televangelists and our other entertainers toward the planet's various neighborhoods in which most of us live, we can see it. Not everywhere perhaps, but at least here and there. We should not be discouraged by this, though. A democratic politics has always been the exception, and its flowering into mass movements more exceptional still. To ask whether we can hope for it, and to be able to answer in the affirmative, it is enough to recognize that it happens, and that it is happening now, in a world dominated by an ideology that has no place for it.

Moreover, the ideal of equality, although pushed to the margins by neoliberal globalization, is not dead. It remains with us, even when it is put to cynical use by those politicians who invoke it in order to justify a current political system or the virtues of the capitalist market. Piven and Cloward rightly note that poor people's movements are constrained by the institutional order in which they take place. This does not mean that they can do no more than reflect that order, but rather that "the opportunities for defiance are structured by features of institutional life."[19] There are social and political contexts that lend themselves to change or resistance, for any number of reasons: instability, corruption, discrimination, dishonesty. And the types of resistance that are open are themselves structured by the context in which they take place. Elected politicians who are skilled at co-opting resistance, for instance, will be difficult to struggle against with open confrontation. None of this means, however, that resistance cannot succeed. What it means is that resistance and struggle take place and must respond to the contingencies of the situation in which they arise.

But there is one aspect of the institutional life of many societies, and of all Western societies, that can help ground resistance. It is the nominal commitment of these societies to the value of equality. Even though neoliberal globalization promotes inequality, and even though it undercuts solidarity and seeks to turn political into economic struggle, it does not reject openly the value of equality. As we saw at the outset of this book, Amartya Sen claimed that all liberal theories that have stood the test of time have promoted an equality of something. Whether that equality is of liberty, resources, opportunity, capabilities, or something else, whatever is held to be of significance to a human life is held to be something to which we must have equal access. Equality provides the framework for thinking about justice in social life.

We also saw that equality is often thought of as something to be distributed rather than to be enacted or expressed through collective action. However, regardless of its being mistakenly or unfortunately conceived, equality remains a value that founds political thought. Even those who embrace neoliberal globalization most wholeheartedly will justify their view by reference to equality: equality of opportunity or equal access to participation in the market. Equality is the great justifier. Nobody can be against it. Even where it is anemically conceived, even where it is violated in the deed, it is nonetheless always pressed into service in favor of one policy or another.

Some might say that this is exactly the problem with equality. It does too much work. It has become empty of content by being invoked so often. This is to mistake its potential. Equality, while stretched to cover egregious arrangements and narrowed to cover too few, remains a powerful value. The goal is not to critique or to abandon it, but to harness it. This is the center of Rancière's project. We must re-appropriate equality from those who would take it from us, either in their words or through their policies. We must wrest equality from the empty rhetoric of elected politicians, save it from the radically inegalitarian policies of neoliberal globalization, and make it work again in favor of those who have the most to gain from it: the part that has no part, whoever and wherever that part might be.

The only way to accomplish this is to appropriate the concept not only in our rhetoric but also in our action. We cannot demand it from others – or not simply demand it from others – but must place it at the center of our own action. Equality cannot be entrusted to the part that already has a part. They will never see their way to an understanding of what equality is or at least what it can be. They have no motivation to do so. At most, as Rancière tells us, they can be mobilized to hear those who act out of the presupposition of their own equality.

The preserve of equality must exist in the collective action of those who presuppose it. Against neoliberal globalization and its apologists, equality becomes the value that can join people together in solidarity, but only if the people, the demos, first and foremost, invoke it in discourse and in organizing. One can ask for equality and equal recognition: we have seen that done by the Algerian immigrants of Montréal and the peasants of southern Mexico. One can demand equality from those who govern, or who benefit at one's expense. However, what one cannot do is cede the conception and implementation of equality to them. Those who seek it must sustain it in their own work. Only then will those who struggle properly recognize one another and properly act on their own and one another's behalf. Equality will retain its content only if it is those who act who give it its content, rather than entrusting it to those whose interests lie elsewhere.

That equality remains a live value can be seen in at least two of the case studies we have followed. In the case of Montréal's Algerian refugees, the movement inspired large segments of the wider Québécois population to support demands for full citizenship. In many ways, as one supporter of the movement told me, the Québécois saw themselves in the Algerian refugees: as people living among others who did not consider them equal. When one of the refugees told me that he was a human being rather than a piece of paper, what was he doing other than claiming his equality? Such claims still have the power to inspire. On a larger stage, the Zapatista resistance has demonstrated the power that remains associated with the assertion of equality. Cutting through the isolationism of identity politics, the Zapatistas reached out and asked the world's various progressive movements to support them in their struggle. This struggle, they explained, was not simply a local struggle for indigenous rights, although it was that as well. It was, and is, at the same time a vision of equality, of people acting on their own behalf, asserting their own dignity. It is no accident that the Zapatista struggle has been one of the most studied, most recognized, and, from the mainstream press and the right, most derided movements of the past several decades. It embraces an equality that can only be a threat to the part that has a part, and that intends to hold onto it.

If, then, Piven and Cloward are right that struggle must always take place within the institutional contexts in which it arises, it is also true that the value associated with a democratic politics is still to be found in those contexts. We do not need to reach outside our current situation in order to discover the normative source for struggle. We have, instead, to invoke it, and to make it work. We have to integrate it into the politics we create.

But what of this politics? Where are we to find it, and how are we to create it in the context of neoliberal globalization? The value may be there, but how can it be expressed under the conditions we have described here?

It is easy, but not too easy, to say that it is already being expressed. It is being expressed in the cases we have described here. In Montréal, in Palestine, in southern Mexico, in rural South Carolina, in Oakland, California, and in many places we have not described, various forms of democracy are in play. We may say that none of these movements has turned into anything like a mass movement. None of them, with perhaps the exceptions of the first intifada and the Zapatista movements in their early moments, has garnered the kind of support or swept across larger segments of the planet's population in ways analogous to the movements of the 1930s or 1960s. While this is true, we must also recognize that democratic movements are alive. They exist. They are being created on the ground, by people whose names we will never hear but who are not afraid to claim their equality with those whose names we cannot rid ourselves of. One of the tasks of this book has been to call attention to contemporary democratic movements that often take place outside the glare of the spectacle the media places before us.

But it is also true, and it has been the burden of this chapter to puzzle over it, that there are currently no mass movements of the kind one might hope for. Perhaps the closest movement or movements to a mass one are the various environmental struggles. These struggles are important and necessary, even though many of them are not democratic struggles in the sense we have described here. (Although some of them are so, as we have seen with the food co-op.) They are not always collective actions that express the presupposition of equality.

We must face the lack of mass democratic movements squarely. We must ask why we do not have them, and how we might create them.

In doing so, it is again easy, but not too easy, to point out that periods of such mass movements are rare. Rancière has pointed to the rarity of democratic politics (although I would prefer to call it the rarity of *mass democratic movements*), and Piven and Cloward are sober about the emergence of poor people's movements. We cannot use this fact as an excuse. But in recognizing it, we can also prevent self-flagellation for the lack of a mass movement. The powers arrayed against democracy are always strong. They bring to bear powerful resources against perceived threats, and the presupposition of equality is surely a threat to any police order. In our time, as we have seen, there is also the difficulty of resistance reaching its target. The distance is often too great for resistance to feel itself to be mobilizing an obligation to hear.

We should not forget this, but neither should we use it as an excuse. We cannot throw up our hands, neither those of us who seek a part nor those in solidarity with them. We must recognize that the appearance of democratic politics is contingent. We have seen that, at least in Piven and Cloward's view, there are contexts in which poor people's movements are more likely to appear. However, we have also seen that in order for movements to appear, there must be a decision – and eventually a collective decision – to act. Movements of struggle and resistance do not simply lie at the end of a causal chain of circumstances. Circumstances may motivate the decision to resist, but they do not cause it. This decision, especially when it is a democratic one, must arise in one way or another from the demos.

The contingency of democratic politics, and the rarity of mass democratic movements, should not lead us to fatalism or despair. The lesson of the contingency of political movements is not that we cannot incite or affect them, or that we must await their appearance. It is precisely that we do not know when and how they appear. That is what contingency means. When a group of Algerian refugees began to meet to discuss their response to Minister Coderre's lifting of the moratorium on their return to Algeria, certainly none of them knew where their actions would lead. None of them had reason, given the history and structure of the Algerian immigrant community in Canada, to expect that they would be able to gather support from their own community, much less that of Québécois society. They did what any reasonable people would do under the circumstances: they talked among themselves, and to others, and sought to create a collective response.

Why did this particular immigration rights movement succeed while others failed? It was not simply that the circumstances were ripe for success. Nor was it simply that there was a collective decision to act. Without these, there would have been no movement, and no success. But neither did their combination guarantee success. We cannot look into their situation and find the keys to social change. If we were able to do that, there would be no police orders, no undemocratic hierarchies. Sometimes movements arise when the circumstances are right, and sometimes they don't. Sometimes they succeed, and sometimes they don't. These things cannot be predicted in advance, or in most cases even during the period of struggle. History can teach us lessons, but it cannot offer us formulas.

The lesson for progressive politics is this: rather than becoming fatalistic, we must instead be vigilant. We must seek to understand the circumstances we are in, look for political openings, educate one another, support the democratic brush fires that arise here and there. Will any of this result in a democratic movement, mass or otherwise? Or instead will these be exercises in failure, efforts that lead nowhere? We don't know. We do not know what will happen if we insert ourselves into the political arena, stand among or alongside the part that has no part. We do not know whether our actions will mobilize an obligation to hear. But we do know what will happen if we do not act. We know this because it is our world; it is the police order that governs us.

Rancière has offered us a framework from within which to think about a democratic politics, a framework that responds to our time. He has not offered us a recipe for change, or a prediction about when it will come about. In fact, his framework explains to us why we cannot have these things. The case studies we have followed here have shown us that, to one degree or another, a democratic politics is possible in our time. A couple of these case studies have also suggested that it might be possible, at least on a local level, to institutionalize a democratic politics. In two cases – that of the first intifada and the Zapatistas – we have even seen glimpses of broad international identification and support. None of these movements has shaken neoliberal globalization to its foundations. But all of them have provided alternative visions for carrying out our collective lives.

Democratic politics is not dead, simply because it is never dead. It is neither dead nor alive. Rather, it comes to life, here and there, when the circumstances are right and people are decided. The project then, for those for whom democracy matters, is not to pronounce upon its fate nor to seek its Archimedean point. It is instead what it has always been: to be ready to engage it, to create it, alongside others with whom one stands and with whom one may share nothing else but equality.

Notes

1   Berger, John (text) and Mohr, Jean (photographs), *A Seventh Man: Migrant Workers in Europe*, New York: Viking Press, 1975, p. 141.
2   Foucault, Michel, "Revolutionary Action: 'Until Now,'" in Donald F. Bouchard (ed.), *Language, Counter-Memory, Practice*, tr. Donald F. Bouchard and Sherry Simon, Ithaca, NY: Cornell University Press, 1977 (or. pub. 1971), pp. 230–1.
3   Piven, Francis Fox, and Cloward, Richard A., *Poor People's Movements: Why They Succeed, How They Fail*, New York: Pantheon, 1977, p. 28.
4   Piven and Cloward, *Poor People's Movements*, p. 14.
5   Piven and Cloward, *Poor People's Movements*, p. 20.
6   Freeman, Alan, "Globalization: Economic Stagnation and Divergence," http://mpra.ub.uni-muenchen.de/6745.
7   Marfleet, Phil, "Globalisation and the Third World," *International Socialism Journal*, issue 81, winter 1998, http://pubs.socialistreview index.org.uk/isj81/marfleet.htm.
8   Marfleet, "Globalisation and the Third World."
9   For more on this, see Stiglitz, Joseph, *Globalization and its Discontents*, New York: W. W. Norton, 2002, and especially Klein, Naomi, *The Shock Doctrine: The Rise of Disaster Capitalism*, New York: Metropolitan Books, 2007.
10   Chang, Ha-Joon, *Bad Samaritans: The Myth of Free Trade and the Secret History of Capitalism*, London: Bloomsbury Press, 2008, p. 28.
11   May, Todd, "Rancière in South Carolina," in Gabrid Rockhill and Philip Watts (eds.), *Jacques Rancière: History, Politics, Aesthetics*, Durham, NC: Duke University Press, 2009.
12   *Disagreement*, p. 33.
13   Piven and Cloward, *Poor People's Movements*, p. 23.
14   Rancière, Jacques, *Hatred of Democracy*, tr. Steve Corcoran, London: Verso, 2006 (or. pub. 2005), p. 81.

15 *On the Shores of Politics*, p. 13.
16 See Barber, Benjamin, *Jihad Vs. McWorld: How the Planet is Both Falling Apart and Coming Together and What This Means for Democracy*, New York: Crown Publishers, 1995.
17 Smith, Adam, *Selections from The Wealth of Nations*, ed. George Stigler, New York: Appleton-Century-Crofts, 1957, p. 11.
18 *Disagreement*, p. 12.
19 Piven and Cloward, *Poor People's Movements*, p. 23.

Index